HOPE
IN THE MIDST OF SHADOWS

ISBN 978-1-909751-73-6

The entire proceeds of this book will be dedicated to the
Life and Learning Fund for Pastors and Students in Romania.

Further copies can be obtained from dr.hamilton.moore@gmail.com *or*
Church Office, Coleraine Baptist Church, Abbey Street, Coleraine, BT52 1EX.

Printed by J.C. Print Ltd.   email: info@jcprint.net

HOPE

in the midst of shadows

Dr Hamilton Moore

Dedication

*This book is dedicated to the members and friends
of the churches where I ministered for over fifty years:
Magherafelt Baptist Church, Monkstown Baptist Church,
Glenarm Baptist Church and Castlereagh Baptist Church.*

Preface

HAVE YOU EVER reached the point when you feel all hope is gone? Plans have been dashed; you have been overcome through an unexpected trial or turn of events; or you have lost someone and feel your life is empty and without meaning; things have become stressful because of situations and you feel like running away. The shadows of life have blotted out the sun. Yet there is "hope." In Rom. 15:4[1] Paul assures us that the things written beforehand were written so that "through endurance and through the encouragement of the Scriptures we might have hope." Some translations have the "comfort of the Scriptures." That is fine, provided we understand that the word "comfort" is not just about sympathy or empathy but about imparting strength or real encouragement in all the various experiences of trial. With such encouragement we can go on in our Christian life. The next verse (v.5) reminds us that it is God himself who is "the God of endurance and encouragement." He is the one who gives us help to endure through his word and brings us "hope."

What is this hope about which Paul writes? It is not an uncertain hope, something of which we cannot be sure. It is more the idea of anticipation; something written for us of which we are certain, rejoice in, and draw our strength from. Here we have one of the reasons why God has given us his word. As you read this book, you will find comfort in what God has assured us of, promises of the "God who never lies," Tit.1:2. All the promises of God in the Lord Jesus Christ "find their Yes in him" to which we can respond and "utter our Amen to God for his glory," 2 Cor. 1:20.

---

[1] Quotations, unless otherwise stated, are taken from the English Standard Version, (Wheaton, Illinois: Crossway, 2001).

It is true as Job in his wisdom reminds us, that man is "born to trouble," 5:7 and his days can be "full of trouble", 14:1. Just as the sun does not always shine and the threatening clouds can come – life can and will have its dark shadows. After 50 years of ministry and personal contact with people I know this to be true. I have often looked down from the pulpit into faces which from all appearances harboured no concerns. But I was aware that in every situation or family somewhere there was disappointment, concern, sadness or pain. How could I help them? I am convinced that the source of our "hope" is found in the Word of God. When life throws so many things your way, different situations, circumstances, losses, your sure rock will be what God has promised.

Isaiah received a two-fold call. First, a call to warn of coming judgment, "until cities lie waste without inhabitant, and houses without people," Isa. 6:11. The problem was that the people were going to harden their hearts. The result was the exile to Babylon. Then in Isa. 40:1 he was given a second commission, "Comfort, comfort my people, says your God." In the darkness and grief of the exile which was still future, Isaiah was to write "prophetically" for them; to bring them hope. This book has been born out of such conviction; the need to comfort God's people to bring hope, the certainty of the Scriptures in the many changing scenes of life. The title chosen "Hope in the Midst of Shadows" contains an important message. All that life throws at us are in a very real sense only shadows and shadows cannot hurt us! Through the God of endurance and encouragement and by trusting in his word we can overcome. We remember the words of David in Psa. 42:5-6, "Why are you cast down, O my soul, and why are you in turmoil within me? Hope in God; for I shall again praise him, my salvation and my God." Also the comfort of the Lord Jesus to his disciples in the upper room before he left them, "I have said these things to you, that in me you may have peace. In the world you will have tribulation. But take heart; I have overcome the world," (John 16:33).

The following chapters are based on messages delivered at various times over fifty years of ministry. They will cover a range of topics; 1 Pet.1:6 says we can be "grieved by various trials." The contents have not been drastically changed but included largely as delivered. In presenting their message I have tried to include scripture quotations, attempting also to acknowledge sources wherever possible.

There is a saying attributed to the Maori people, which is often quoted; if you turn your face towards the sun, the shadows fall behind you. Generally it is used to affirm the value of optimism. One recalls the wisdom also of Proverbs 15:13, "A glad heart makes a cheerful face, but by sorrow of heart the spirit is crushed." This book claims that it is through our all-sufficient God and his sure word that we can dispel the shadows. Or if we turn our faces towards the "Son" we can go on in the midst of them, in the darkness they cast across our path, until finally, the "shadows flee away." Standing somewhere in the shadows of life, we can find Jesus.

Contents

Foreword

MORE THAN EVER when we look at our needy world we get a sense of despair and hopelessness. Where are we going, what on earth is happening? Is there any answer to the many problems that we face? With regard to Christian living we sometimes feel that everything is too big for us. An old preacher once put it like this. "There are three big problems that we face: Anarchy in the world, Apostasy in the professing church and Apathy in the evangelical church." He then went on to underscore that the third problem was the biggest!! It is apathy that can rob us of a genuine hope. In the Psalter, (the Scottish Metrical view of the Psalms), we read "When darkness doth come." Psalm 104: 20. There is darkness, but hope can overcome the most difficult of experiences.

My good friend Hamilton Moore has written this book to lift our spirits, enlighten our minds and above all to encourage our hope in our Eternal Lord. He, in a very practical, helpful and biblical way, asks us to allow the word of God to encourage and build us up in our faith. You will also capture, through his many years of pastoral and personal experience, the glorious hope that faith in our Lord Jesus Christ brings. Years ago someone wrote "Hope is a good thing, maybe the best of things and no good thing will ever die." I know you will be blessed and encouraged by this timely book and find Hope in the Midst of Shadows. "The Light shines through the darkness, and the darkness can never extinguish it" John 1:5. N.L.T.

Pastor Val English

CHAPTER ONE

Hope When God Seems Far Off

Isaiah 57:1-21

ARE YOU FEELING lonely and does God seem to be far away? Remember our personal, private feelings can deceive. God is never far away. We have his promise in this passage.

The first part of the chapter sets out the picture of Israel's rebellion against God when they were taken away in the Babylonian captivity in 587 BCE and God's openness to forgive the repentant soul. Here we may have a picture of the type of godlessness which was seen in Manasseh's reign.

vv. 1-2 The righteous man "perishes" and the devout are "taken away": they are taken away through violence and persecution. Leaders do not care; but we read that, "he enters into peace."

vv. 3-13 The ungodly are facing judgment. God sets before us through Isaiah his prophet a catalogue of sins. They were addicted to sorcery, fertility rites, and "slaughter their children" to false gods like the god Molech, worshipping stones from the river that looked like gods, flattering foreign kings. God was longsuffering. The question is who will help them when the invader comes, when they are taken away? "When you cry out, let your collection of idols deliver you! The wind will carry them off, a breath will take them away," (v.13). Yet God holds out hope for the future beyond the Captivity.

vv. 14-19 God would not remain angry forever; he will find a way to accept them. From Babylon a believing remnant will return. God graciously will "remove every obstruction" from his people's way; there would be a great turning to him; he will restore the contrite in heart.

It is in this context that we can find our hope when God seems far away. In v.15 there are three great truths about God:

WHO GOD IS
"For thus says the One who is high and lifted up, who inhabits eternity, whose name is Holy."

God is high and lifted up. We remember Isa. 40 which affirms he rules far above all; he is sovereign over every authority and of course every false god. We are reminded also of Isa. 6:1-3. He is "the LORD of Hosts." There is so little recognition of the awesome nature of God today. Here is "the unknown God" of modern Christendom. But this great God is your God.

He inhabits eternity. He is the eternal God. He is beyond time. In Psa. 102:25-27 we read "Of old you laid the foundation of the earth, and the heavens are the work of your hands. They will perish, but you will remain; they will all wear out like a garment. You will change them like a robe, and they will pass away, but you are the same, and your years have no end." He is the first and he is the last. Psa. 90:2 also affirms, "Before the mountains were brought forth, or ever you had formed the earth and the world, from everlasting to everlasting you are God."

He is Holy. Holiness is his essential character. Separated, unlike all others. Intrinsically holy.

WHERE GOD DWELLS
"I dwell in the high and holy place."

We may think this refers to heaven. There is such a place above and beyond the atmospheric heavens and the stellar heavens. But neither the "heaven" or the "earth" can contain him, Isa. 66:1, Acts 7:48-49. So God dwells in the spiritual dimension beyond time and space. He is the transcendent God. But this is where we can find comfort for the text affirms that he also dwells "with him who is of a contrite and lowly spirit." You can see that it would apply to those God was reaching out to in Babylon who felt forsaken and far away from their former home. Isa. 40:27 tells us, "Why do you say, O Jacob, and speak, O Israel, 'My way is hidden from the Lord, and my right is disregarded by my God?'" Again Isaiah records in Isa. 49:14, "But Zion said, 'The LORD has forsaken me; my Lord has forgotten me.'" Is this also true of you? Do you feel forsaken and does it seem that God is far away?

Let me assure you that the God who is transcendent, who "sits above the circle of the earth," Isa. 40:22, whose ways are "higher than your ways" and whose thoughts are higher than your thoughts, Isa. 55:9, is also "a God at hand…and not a God far away," Jer. 23:23 and so is also imminent within his creation. Isa. 6:3 declares that "the whole earth is full of his glory!" and he is "the God of the whole earth," Isa. 54:5. He is a God who is near us, who "will tend his flock like a shepherd; he will gather the lambs in his arms; he will carry them in his bosom, and gently lead those that are with young," Isa. 40:11. He cannot do this from a distance! He can give power to the faint, Isa. 40:29.

The truth of God's imminence assures us that God is present in all of creation, while remaining distinct from it. In other words, there is no place where God is not. His sovereign control extends everywhere simultaneously. But he is here – that is the point.

WHAT GOD DOES

He is here "to revive the spirit of the lowly, and to revive the heart of the contrite."

Has your heart felt cold these past days? Sin in our lives can destroy our communion with God. David confesses in Psa. 32:3-4, "For when I kept silent, my bones wasted away through my groaning all day long. For night and day your hand was heavy upon me; my strength was dried up as by the heat of summer." God invites you to return to him. All that is required is that you come with a contrite and humble spirit. God, the almighty God, the high and lofty one, will forgive and he can dwell with you. See also Isa. 66:1-2. The Lord tells us that he is truly transcendent; "Thus says the LORD: 'Heaven is my throne, and earth is my footstool.'" But he promises, "this is the one to whom I will look: he who is humble and contrite in spirit and trembles at my word." What a great God we have! While the heaven of heavens is not too great for him to dwell in, the human heart is not too small.

But perhaps it is not through some sinful act. You feel forsaken; problems unsurmountable; shadows surround you and God seems so far away; you are in total despair. God knows exactly where you are and how you feel. He is closer than your heartbeat. Draw near to him in prayer and he will draw near to you. If you call upon him … he can revive your spirit! He has gracious plans for you…Psa. 136:23 assures us that he remembers us in our "low estate." He has promised never to leave you nor forsake you, Heb. 13:5. There are five negatives in the original Greek text i.e., "I will never, no never, no never leave go of your hand." A young minister pointed this out to an old Christian lady as he read to her this verse from the Scriptures and prayed with her – the Lord's promise was confirmed five times. He received the reply, "Once is good enough for me." In the midst of the shadows he will be enough for you and by faith you will find him.

CHAPTER TWO

Hope When You are Troubled and Confused

Isaiah 40:12-31

THINGS HAPPEN WHICH we cannot and do not understand. Our minds question "Why has God allowed this to happen to me?" "Does God not know? Does he not see?" We are confused and bewildered. We return to a passage touched upon in the last chapter. God has a word for us – which once was a word to the exiles who were in Babylon.

Isaiah was an 8th century BCE prophet who prophesied in Jerusalem in the land of Judah, right up until the time of Hezekiah's reign. As we read in the Preface to this work, Isaiah received a two-fold commission, Isa. 6:8-13. He was to call the people to repentance; but they did not heed his preaching and were only hardened by it. Later when Hezekiah was sick, God had mercy on the king and he recovered. In Isa. 39:1-8 the son of the king of Babylon sent envoys with a present. He no doubt had a strategy to cement a friendship which might help him against Assyria. Hezekiah welcomed them, showed the visitors his wealth and his heart was lifted up with pride in this human patronage. He was ready to form an alliance with the king of Babylon rather than trust in God. Isaiah the prophet goes to him and announces that one day "all that is in your house, and that which your fathers have stored up till this day" would be taken down to Babylon; also "some of your own sons, who will come from you," (Isa. 39:6-8). Hezekiah's recorded response is that he is relieved that it will not happen in his own day! Isaiah however carried the burden for Judah home with him and God so spoke to him. He learned that he could write as if he was there 150 years ahead and speak to those in that dreadful experience of the captivity. Isa. 40 is where the transition in time begins.

THERE ARE CAPTIVES here. v. 12f

Isaiah's prophecy has come true. The people are in exile. Isa. 40 is a call to comfort those in distress, those who are confused and feel that God has forgotten or is unaware of their circumstances. Here we have the precious theme of the greatness of God, vv. 12-31.

THERE IS CONFUSION here. v.27

Isaiah reflects the questionings of the exiles who are tempted to accept that God must not see them where they are. He must only be a local God. If he knew their just cause he would deal with it. God speaks to them, "Why do you say O Jacob, and speak O Israel, 'My way is hidden from the Lord and my right is disregarded by my God?'" (The reference to "Jacob" the supplanter is likely used because he was out of fellowship with God at times, out of his homeland and in a distant country). The people in Babylon were confused and wondering what God was doing or could do about their situation. Does he not see? Why should this happen to us? These are questions which have been asked many times by God's people in different circumstances.

THERE IS COMFORT here. v.1 and v.12f

Isaiah shows us God the incomparable. Here we have a mighty revelation which rebukes our small ideas about God.

God and his WORLD vv. 12-15

The captives were exhorted to grasp his almighty power and wisdom. Isaiah challenged them to reflect on the one who has "measured the waters in the hollow of his hand" and who "marked off the heavens with a span." We can hold very little in the hollow of our hands – perhaps a little water to quench our thirst. Two thirds of the earth's surface is covered by water much of it made up of the world's great oceans. Isaiah presents God as the one who in creative power can hold it all in his hand! He can then certainly hold us! Turning from the waters to the mighty heavens again Isaiah asks us to consider God's greatness. Think of the vastness of the universe with its galaxies and clusters of stars! He measured it we are told with the span of his hand! Isaiah reminds us that the Spirit of God consulted with no-one in the great work of creation. The nations, the most populous and the most powerful, are compared to "the drop from a bucket" and like the "dust on the scales" which will be disregarded in taking even the smallest measurement. Compared with them, what can such a great God not do?

God and his WORSHIP vv.16-25
Such a God is worthy of the highest worship. We are reminded of the great forests of Lebanon with its mighty cedars and the unnumbered beasts which roam through them. Neither the wood from its many cedars nor the multitude of beasts could provide a sufficient offering to bring to him! They try to make an image of God and through the skill of the craftsman it is overlaid with the best gold and the silver chains are attached. But he can never be represented like this. He is the sovereign God who "sits above the circle of the earth" and the one who can bring down the most mighty from their thrones.

God and his WORKS vv. 26-28
The captives as we noted may think at times that God does not know or see; but he does. Isaiah encourages us to look up again at the night sky, the starry heavens which God created. In v.26, he lines them up like a mighty army but the most amazing affirmation is that he knows the individual characteristic of every star. He knows their number and their names – to the farthest reaches of outer space. He not only knows them but he keeps them in place! "Because he is strong in power not one is missing."

When they are tempted to think that God does not know or see, they need to remember that their God is not limited by TIME. He is "the everlasting God". He has not some kind of TERRITORIAL LIMITATION. He is the "Creator of the ends of the earth." He is not wearied by EFFORT for "he does not faint". Nor does he suffer from any LACK OF KNOWLEDGE "his understanding is unsearchable" (v.28).

Such a great God can give power to the faint and strength to those who are without strength, (v.29).

THERE IS CONFIDENCE here v. 31

Isaiah gives them an exhortation, "wait for the Lord" or as NIV "hope" in the Lord. AV translates "wait upon the Lord." So is the exhortation for us to pray? This could be part of it but the emphasis appears different. The word really means to "trust"; it signifies patient expectation or waiting for God. The captives or exiles in their desperate plight must trust in God. And so must we. We can:

TRUST in his OVER-RULING PURPOSE

He is working out his purpose although we may not see it now. To Peter in John 13:7 Jesus could say "What I am doing you do not understand now, but afterward you will understand." He had a plan for the captives. He is still in control today whatever your circumstances are.

TRUST in his JUSTICE

We must remember that evil will not go unpunished. As far as Judah was concerned, the Lord sent "persistently" his messengers to them but they mocked and despised them "until there was no remedy," 2 Chron. 36:16. So God used Babylon to bring just judgment upon them, but then finally punished them also for their brutality.

TRUST in his SUSTAINING GRACE

Even the youths faint-the choicest, the fittest will become weary. We can faint at the throne of grace. Luke 18:1 reminds us that we ought always to pray and not to faint; we can faint in the path of service. Gal. 6:9 urges us not to grow weary in doing good, for in due season we shall reap if we do not faint; we can faint on the road of life. In Hebrews 12:5 where the author encourages us not to despise …nor faint when we are rebuked by him; we can faint in the problems of the way. In 2 Cor. 4:16 Paul tells us that though our outward man perish, our inward man is renewed day by day. As we look to God and by faith lean upon him, we do not faint or lose heart.

The everlasting God does not faint…gives power to the faint…so that we can walk and not faint. He can uphold you, help you to meet all the demands of life. Looking to him, he can "renew your strength"; you can be upheld, receive confidence to continue – even in the hardest place of all, through all the daily routine of life. You can "walk and not faint". Rely upon him from day to day.

Do you know this God? The whole world is in his hands. He is working his purpose out. Trust him. He can sustain you every day, in the bright days and the dark days. You will find him still in the shadows.

CHAPTER THREE

Hope in Days of Lonliness

Isaiah. 49:1-16 Engraved on the Palms of His Hands

BRITAIN HAS BEEN CALLED the capital of lonliness in all of Europe. This can be true anywhere in the world. Times of lonliness are journeys in which we come face to face with the reality of emotional and mental pain. Yet in the secret corners of our shattered expectations, in the moments of quietness when the silence is deafening and the shadows close in around us, God offers his promise of hope. The following verses contain different themes for us to consider:

There are Themes which are Christological

The chapter begins with a Servant passage. Sometimes it is clear that the passage speaks of Israel, "You are my servant, Israel, in whom I will be glorified," v.3. But the Servant also has a mission to Israel and in fact to the whole world. "And now the LORD says, he who formed me from the womb to be his servant, to bring Jacob back to him; and that Israel might be gathered to him - for I am honoured in the eyes of the LORD, and my God has become my strength - he says 'It is too light a thing that you should be my servant to raise up the tribes of Jacob and to bring back the preserved in Israel; I will make you as a light for the nations, that my salvation may reach to the end of the earth,'" vv.5-7. We can say that the Servant can be in certain passages Israel idealised, or all that God intended Israel to be. But ultimately here the fulfilment is in Christ and his sacrificial service. Note also v.8a "Thus says the Lord: 'In a time of favor I have answered you; in a day of salvation I have helped you...'" is quoted by Paul in 2 Cor. 6:2 as fulfilled in the coming of the Lord Jesus and his saving work. So Christ was the one called with a mission to Israel and the whole world; his mouth was as a sharp sword and having known the unresponsiveness of the nation, he leaves his work with God, (49:2-4).

There are Statements that are Prophetical

The passage has references that focus prophetically on Israel. In vv.8-13 the "prisoners" flocking home are visualized as the dispersed of Israel throughout the world, not merely from Babylon v.12, "these shall come from afar…" and v.22 "Thus says the Lord LORD: 'Behold, I will lift up my hand to the nations, and raise my signal to the peoples; and they shall bring your sons in their bosom, and your daughters shall be carried on their shoulders.'"

Some see here fulfilment ONLY in the Church made up of Jews and Gentiles; but the literal references in e.g., v.12 "these shall come from afar, and behold, these from the north and from the west, and these from the land of Syene," can point to a yet future fulfilment for national Israel. AT THE PRESENT only Christian Jews are right with God – the Jewish believers in the Middle East and throughout the world. But the nation is back in unbelief. The veil is upon their minds when Moses is read. They are godless and can be brutal. They will be held accountable to God. They are returning from even the land of Syene (Lower Egypt) or the suggested variant name Sinum (China or even the Russian Jews of whom there are many in Palestine) and one day God will reveal himself again to them.

There are Elements which are Historical

We can see that there are verses that relate to the situation in Isaiah's day with the prophet foreseeing the distress of the exiles in Babylon – "forsaken" and "forgotten," vv.14-16. But as Zion cries out and is pictured as a woman bereft of husband and children, God speaks to assure her she has not been forsaken nor forgotten, as vv.15-16 will affirm. In fact her best days are before her when her new family will overflow all bounds, the former "waste" and "desolate places" will be "too narrow" to dwell in, vv.19-20. We are reminded of the "Jerusalem above" teaching of Gal.4:25-27, Jews and Gentiles in Christ the true children of Abraham. These statements were meant to assure the exiles of God's unfailing love. But we can also say that:

There are Promises which can be Personal
God's promises are here as in many other parts of Scripture and we can apply them to ourselves. As we have seen, the first part of this chapter is a Servant Song. It is not just Israel, but an individual, the Servant of the Lord, see v.1, "The LORD called me from the womb." The deliverer is one infinitely greater than Cyrus. He is commissioned. Now we see as the chapter continues that the people thought that God had "forsaken" and "forgotten" them, v.14. Remember when they were in Babylon, and they were lamenting that their way must be hidden from him or he must not know their just cause or he would help them, Isa. 40:27. Here in v.14 the first verb suggests an outward abandoning, the second an inner forsaking. Sounds familiar? Do you have such feelings? As far as Zion was concerned, she believed that she was utterly forsaken by her God. Their weakness was real; they were little and insignificant. But to them promises were given. They are also for you.

YOU ARE IN HIS MIND
"can a woman forget…yet I will not forget you," (v.15). Sometimes a mother can give birth in a hospital in Romania and the following morning she is gone and her child is abandoned. The reason is often that she cannot feed any more children. Perhaps she will never forget her child but even if "these may forget" the Lord promises "yet will I not forget you." You are never forgotten.

YOU ARE ON HIS HANDS
"Behold, I have engraved you upon the palms of my hands," (v.16). You are precious to him. What a promise! Let us consider this statement further.

THE PROCLAMATION

"Behold." He means, "Consider this!" "Take note," "Remember this." We so quickly forget! God has in his infinite mercy to remind us again and again. Do you need reminded? Often when trouble comes and the shadows of life envelop us, we do.

THE PERFORMANCE

"I have" When God does something who can undo it or frustrate his purpose? In Rom. 8:28-30 Paul focuses upon "those who are called according to his purpose." He states in v.30 "those whom he predestined he also called, and those whom he called he also justified, and those whom he justified he also glorified." There is an unbroken chain in God's purpose; so Paul can write about the justified as glorified, using the past tense. In vv.38-39 he is "sure" that neither death (which is a great separator), nor life (with all its problems), nor angels nor rulers (the unseen host of good and evil), even things as they are at present, nor all that is to come, whatever it may be, nor anything in height or depth, in fact, throughout all of creation, "will be able to separate us from the love of God in Christ Jesus our Lord."

THE PERMANENCE

"engraved." Not written, but engraved. I sometimes write on my hand when I have something important to remember. God does not simply write them – they are engraved – it is permanent! It cannot be removed! Therefore, you are always there before him. As Spurgeon[2] has explained:

> These words seem to say to us that God has already secured, beyond any possible hazard, his tender memory towards all his own. He has done this in such a way that forgetfulness can never occur at any moment whatsoever. The memorial is not set up in heaven, for then you might

---

[2]   C.H. Spurgeon, "Neither Forsaken nor Forgotten," Nov. 5 1882 in www.preceptaustin.org accessed July 2017.

conceive that God could descend, and leave that memorial. It is not
written upon Almighty's skirts, to speak after the manner of men, - for
he might disrobe himself for conflict, but he has put the token of his
love where it cannot be laid aside – on the palms of his hands.

While a man lives the memorial is there. God is the everlasting
God. He loves us with an everlasting love. He will never forsake you.

THE PEOPLE
"you" His own, you and me. This is for all his covenant people. In
Exod. 28:15-30 we read of "the breastplate of judgment." There
were twelve stones set in it, one for each tribe in Israel, "So Aaron
shall bear the names of the sons of Israel in the breastplate of judgment
on his heart, when he goes into the Holy Place, to bring them to
regular remembrance before the Lord," (28:29). It did not matter that
one tribe was smaller numerically or less important than the other; they
all had the same place upon the High Priest's heart and were
remembered before the Lord. You may consider yourself of little
importance, unknown as far as the kingdom of God is concerned. But
you have the same remembrance before God! You are his special
possession.

THE PLACE
"on the palms of my hands." Is it possible that here we have a little
foreglimpse of what he did for us at Calvary? He has engraved us upon
the palms of his hands in the sense that he died for us; his hands were
pierced for us. He will not now let us go. John 10:28-29 affirms that "I
give them (his sheep) eternal life, and they will never perish, and no one
will snatch them out of my hand. My Father, who has given them to
me, is greater than all, and no one is able to snatch them out of my
Father's hand." Again, in Romans 5:9-11 we have Paul's "much mores"
arguing that if God has done the greater thing for us he will surely do

the lesser. In the past we were "ungodly" (v.6) and "sinners" (v.8); but now our relationship with God is different and we are accepted. "Since, therefore, we have now been justified by his blood, much more shall we be saved by him from the wrath of God." Once we were "enemies" but were then "reconciled to God by the death of his Son." So Paul reasons again, "much more, now that we are reconciled, shall we be saved by his life," (v.10). In fact, we share his risen life and are safe in him.

But this statement concerning his hands surely also reflects the tenderness of God's care for us. The palm is the most tender place. Day by day we continue to experience his tender love, his unfailing expressions of compassion.

THE PROMISE
"Your walls are continually before me". The walls of Zion stand ever before him. He knows their situation and their enemies will not take him by surprise.

Applying this personally to us, we noted already that we were IN HIS MIND AND ON HIS HANDS. Now Isa. 49:16 assures us:

YOU ARE BEFORE HIS EYES
"Your walls are continually before me." You are always before him. You are never out of his sight. How can you think that you are forgotten? When the dark shadows of life envelop you and the darkness of the night gathers around you, you are still "before" him. He sees you where you are. In Genesis 16:13, with Hagar, when the angel of the Lord directed her to return to her mistress she could testify, "Truly here I have seen him who looks after me."

What a great God we have! There are promises which we can make our very own personal possession. Remember that the promises of God in the Scriptures are not just to be "framed," which many do to remind them of them day by day. They are also to be "claimed" in all the difficulties and darkness we face.

YOU ARE IN HIS MIND
"can a woman forget…yet I will not forget you."

YOU ARE ON HIS HANDS
"I have engraved you upon the palms of my hands." You are precious to him.

YOU ARE IN HIS SIGHT
"Your walls are continually before me." He has not forgotten us but we must then not forget him. Moses repeatedly warned the people not to forget the Lord when they were settled in the promised land. "Take care, lest you forget the covenant of the LORD your God, which he made with you, and make a carved image, the form of anything that the LORD your God has forbidden you," Deut. 4:23. How can we forget such a great God who never forgets us? It is having a dynamic relationship with this God day by day that will dispel the shadows.

CHAPTER FOUR

Hope in Situations of Crisis

Hebrews 4:14-16

"HELP" IS THE cry of a heart faced with an unexpected situation or crisis. But where can we expect to find help? Our help is in the Lord; there is hope in him. The gospel story proclaims his death on the cross for sinners. 1 Tim. 1:15 states "Christ Jesus came into the world to save sinners." We could never save ourselves; he came to do for us what we could never accomplish by ourselves. His death on the cross for the hopeless brings forgiveness and acceptance with God when we repent (turn from our sin, our independence of God, our self-confidence to accomplish our own salvation) and put our trust in him.

When we are brought into a saving relationship with Christ he does not abandon us. Heb. 4:16 reminds us there is "grace to help in time of need." The phrase "in time of need" could have been translated "in the nick of time" – the clock may soon strike midnight and the shadows may deepen, but he can come even in the very hour of crisis. He is always there for us, because he was raised from the dead and is able to come to our aid. How can this happen? Hebrews 4:14-16 shows us the way. Christ is set before us as our Great High Priest.

WHERE IS HE NOW?

He "passed through the heavens." Here we have a reference to the heavenly regions in general. Earthly priests had the highest privilege only of passing once a year (for a few moments) through the veil of the tabernacle or temple to appear on behalf of their people. Our Great High Priest ROSE FROM THE DEAD, "presented himself alive" for

FORTY DAYS (Acts 1:2-3), ASCENDED, and now appears for us in the presence of God. Heb. 7:23-24 assures us that while in the past in Israel earthly priests were "prevented by death from continuing in office" by contrast, our Lord Jesus "holds his priesthood permanently, because he continues forever."

In light of this we are urged to "hold fast our confession," 4:14 and 10:23 also urges us to "Let us hold fast the confession of our hope without wavering." The people to whom the Epistle to the Hebrews was first written were going through difficult times, times of crisis. Heb. 10:32-37 speaks of "a hard struggle with sufferings, sometimes publically exposed to reproach and affliction...the plundering of their property" as they were cut off often from other family members and lost their inheritance. They were tempted to give up, but were being urged to go on – because they had a great High Priest. HE WAS THERE FOR THEM IN HEAVEN. In times of crisis he is also there for you.

WHO IS HE?

"Jesus." This is the intentional use of his human name which the author often employs, 2:9; 3:1; 6:20; 7:22; 10:19; 12:24; 13:12. This name occurs as frequently as "Christ." The author of Hebrews is making clear to his readers that the Lord's transcendence has not changed his humanity. The point is that as truly man he knows by experience. He is also "Son of God" affirming his deity. This is the first use of the full title of him in the epistle (only "his Son" in 1:2). It is used again in 6:6; 7:3; 10:29. As human, he knows our pain; as divine, he can do the things we ask – he has the power.

HOW DOES HE FEEL ABOUT US?

The author uses the word "sympathize." If you think that no-one cares about you and your situation you are wrong. He cares!

As far as the first readers are concerned, he has an unequalled ability to sympathize with them – and also with us. He himself has been exposed to life's difficult experiences. This is the reason he can help us. As the author has said already in this Epistle, "Because he himself has suffered when tempted, he is able to help those who are being tempted," (2:17-18).

"Yet without sin" here he reminds us that although humanness as we know it (since the fall) is inherently sinful, it does not follow that sin is intrinsic or essential to humanness. Jesus himself is not just truly God but fully human – without sin. We can come with full confidence. If the readers are going to hold firmly to the faith (v.14), they need to avail themselves of the help that comes from the very presence of God. We remember that when Jesus left his disciples and ascended into heaven, his followers could still reach him – through prayer. In Acts 1:12-14 after the ascension, eleven disciples returned to Jerusalem to the upper room where they were staying. We are then told, "All these with one accord were devoting themselves to prayer, together with the women and Mary the mother of Jesus, and his brothers." They were still in touch with him through the throne of grace! Heb. 4:16 makes it clear that so can you. Your cry "help" will be heard there by him.

WHAT CAN HE DO FOR US?

In v.16 we are encouraged to come to him, because he knows our circumstances and better still understands them. "Let us then with confidence draw near to the throne of grace, that we may receive mercy and find grace to help in time of need." We can "draw near." The epistle is about access to God. Before the coming of Christ the Jewish High Priest could only enter the inner sanctuary of the tabernacle/temple "once a year, and not without taking blood," 9:7. The way was "not yet opened" until Christ offered himself as a sacrifice for sinners and "entered once for all," (9:12) and "sat down at the right hand of God," (10:12). In all their troubles and the crises which they were experiencing the first readers might have been tempted to go back to the temple in Jerusalem (which was still standing) and the High Priest and sacrifices being offered there. But those sacrifices were of no value any longer and could "never take away sins," (10:11). Their High Priest was not in Jerusalem but in heaven and by his death for them they also now share his access; "Therefore, brothers, since we have confidence to enter the holy places by the blood of Jesus," (10:19). The confidence with which they are to come, implies deliverance from fear because of his redemption, because they have been "perfected for all time" (10:14) – his death has the ability to "purify our conscience" (9:14) - and so they enjoy a freedom of expression when they come.

At the throne of grace as the writer emphasises we can "receive mercy" because of the propitiation of 2:17, by which he bears and removes the wrath which we deserved and can accept us when we repent. But he also will, as we pour out our hearts to him, in every crisis give us "grace to help" or what Bruce calls "timely help."[3]

Remember he will be always there for us! In chapter 5 the author shows that he is greater than Aaron. Death removed him and all the "former priests" the "many in number," but as far as your High Priest is concerned, as we noted earlier, he "holds the priesthood permanently," (5:23-24).

We remember the story of an elderly lady when the minister called to see her. The doctor was just leaving and she told her minister that he was the new doctor who had just come to the practice. Her former doctor had died and she confessed, "Mr. Brown my new doctor is very good; but he is not like Mr. Smyth who knew me from my childhood." How precious to know that the one we started the journey with as a believer will be with us all the way even until the end.

Holding fast the confession of our hope without wavering is a key idea in the epistle. In fact Guthrie[4] suggests that these verses in 4:14-

3   F. F. Bruce, *The Epistle to the Hebrews*, NICNT (Grand Rapids, Mich.: W. B. Eerdmans Publishing Company, 1990), 117.

4   D. Guthrie, *The Letter to the Hebrews*, (Leicester, England: Inter-Varsity Press, 1988), 121.

16 may be regarded as the prologue to the High Priestly theme and 10:19f. as the epilogue. In both passages the author encourages us to maintain our confession and draw near to God through our High Priest with confidence. This is part of the structure of the epistle.

It is clear that the interest here is not theoretical, but practical; Jesus is in heaven for us and we have unhindered access to him; we can continue, for he will never fail to give us the grace to go on. The door is open to the throne of grace and at any time or anywhere we can draw near. We have this certain hope in every time of crisis.

Spurgeon[5] in *Morning and Evening* comments upon the text in Zechariah 14:8, "Living waters will flow…in summer and in winter":

> The heats of business cares and scorching trials make me need the cooling influences of the river of His grace; I may go at once and drink to the full from the inexhaustible fountain, for in summer and in winter it pours forth its flood. The upper springs are never scanty…the lower springs cannot fail either.

He refers to the Nile, so important for the survival of the whole nation and the city of Babylon.

> The Nile is the great confidence of Egypt, but its floods are variable; our Lord is the same forever. By turning the course of the Euphrates, Cyrus took the city of Babylon, but no power, human or infernal, can divert the current of divine grace. All of the tracks of ancient rivers have been found dry and desolate, but the streams which take their rise on the mountains of divine sovereignty and infinite love shall ever be full to the brim. Generations melt away, but the course of grace is unaltered.

As the shadows fall across your path in life, all the grace you need is available.

---

[5] Charles Haddon Spurgeon, *Morning and Evening*, (Peabody, MA: Hendrickson Publishers 1998), 366.

CHAPTER FIVE

Hope in Times of Loss

THE TRAUMA OF loss can result from different experiences in life e.g., redundancy; financial ruin; insecurity; sense of helplessness; loss of confidence; reputation; the severing of trusted relationships. But the most common experience of loss comes through bereavement. Dark shadows engulf our paths, huge waves driven by tempestuous winds sweep over us and we feel submerged in deep waters overwhelming us and causing us to sink. It is true that loss through bereavement is the hardest of all to bear mainly because there is a finality about it; there is a recognition of the fact that the earthly existence and precious relationships we have treasured are over. Again, blocked grief can have serious consequences, hindering emotional and even physical well-being.

There are said to be a number of experiences through which the bereaved will generally pass. This has often been referred to as a "grieving process." These can be set out as follows.[6]

IT HASN'T HAPPENED or the denial syndrome.
One can experience absolute unbelief and incredulity as to what has happened.

This can be particularly true if the death was sudden. In course of time eventually disbelief gives way to realism, as the truth sets in, and the bereaved person finally begins to recognise their changed circumstances and come to terms with the sad reality of their loss.

---

[6] Counsellors in bereavement care have often recommended the following book, and reading lists in Pastoral Care modules have also included it; Sydney Callaghan, *Good Grief*, (Newtownards: Colourpoint Books, 1999). Part One, "Stages of Grief: Milestones on the Journey" 15-55, focus on various responses to bereavement. These brief chapters have been helpful in this summary.

IT SHOULDN'T HAVE HAPPENED TO ME or the anger syndrome.

This reaction may very well be totally out of character for the particular individual. Anger may be directed to those nearest and dearest of the bereaved; or it can be self-directed, mixed up with feelings of guilt (see below). Sometimes the anger may be directed toward God. He is the One who has allowed it to happen. But instead of asking "Why me?" should we not be asking "Why not me?"

I MUST ACT AS IF IT HASN'T HAPPENED or the stoic syndrome.

We can bottle up our grief, doubts, and questions. It is possible that it may take a long time before someone's fears, anger, doubts, regrets associated with the death of the particular loved one come to the surface. It is a personal journey, with no set time frame. A journey we all prefer not to travel.

I FEEL BAD THAT IT HAS HAPPENED or the guilt syndrome.

Perhaps there is the remembrance of unfulfilled plans, good intentions, or the loss of the opportunity to put something right. The most important response to bereavement is the last:

IT HAS HAPPENED TO ME or the acceptance syndrome.

With this response we are considering the time when the bereaved "accepts" what has taken place, and begins to respond positively to the changed situation in which he/she finds himself placed. It has often been pointed out that there can still be a difference in time between the one who has suffered this loss acknowledging with the mind what has taken place, and accepting it emotionally. It is best that only when head and heart have come together, is it safe to move on, to take major decisions, or to make major changes. Certainly, it is advisable not to make major decisions within the first year; our mind needs time to settle, to accept that joint decisions are now minus one. Also, one needs to remember that grieving is part of the natural process and is to be expected. One should feel no guilt in this, from a Christian perspective.

The Bible deals with the experience of bereavement realistically. Death is described as "the last enemy" which will one day be destroyed, (1 Cor. 15:26); it is the result of the coming in of sin in the garden of Eden (Gen. 3:17ff.); it means separation and grief for those left behind. But for our loved ones in Christ the Scriptures give us hope. It is true that we still sorrow in bereavement and our grief can be real, but there are assurances about the present circumstances of our loved one and our future reunion. We will look at some passages which can help us in bereavement and give us hope to endure and strength to go on in spite of our loss. One day the shadows will flee away.

2 Cor. 5:1-10. Seeing Things as They Really Are

At times we are very earth bound in our thinking and in our view of what has happened. In other words, we tend to only look at things from an earthly perspective. Yet it can help us if we look at things as they really are. The Scripture here reminds us that we should endeavour to "walk by faith, not by sight."

Paul reminds us that Christians can move from "the tent that is our earthly home" (v.1), a temporary structure vulnerable to the winds of circumstance and to the wear and tear of life to "a building from God," a permanent body or an eternal house designed to last forever. Paul ideally wanted to move directly from one to the other, which would happen if Christ were to actually come. Otherwise he would be in what he calls an "unclothed" state (v. 4) for a while, but still a better state than at present. Elsewhere he can write that "For to me, to live is Christ, and to die is gain" and of being "with Christ, for that is far better," (Phil. 1:21, 23).

The passage here also tells us that when we suffer loss our loved ones move from an existence that is "mortal," in which we groan, to "life" (v. 4), the life of heaven. John Owen as he was close to death said to his secretary, "I am still in the land of the living...no, I am yet in the land of the dying and I hope soon to be in the land of the living."[7]

This is not just some kind of wishful thinking. God has already given us an initial gift, the Holy Spirit who indwells us, what Paul calls in v.5 "the guarantee" of what is to come. So again death is simply a move from the guarantee to the full possession.

Finally, it is a change in v.6 from being "away from the Lord" (not yet with him) to being "at home with the Lord." So Paul explains that in the light of these realities, we should "walk by faith, not by sight," v.7.

When we exercise faith we do not simply look at the circumstances on a natural level. We grasp the fact that our loved ones have passed out of a temporary, mortal state to the perfect life of heaven, from the guarantee or deposit to the full possession. They have gone home. This wonderful passage gives us hope in a time of loss. This hope is also real because of Paul's teaching about the resurrection in 1 Cor. 15:1-58.

First, THE FACT OF THE RESURRECTION

He begins the chapter with a rebuke; 15:1f reminds them that he had preached about the resurrection as part of the good news he had brought to them. They seem to be denying this in some way. He had preached that Christ had been raised and went on to list appearances of Christ. He musters the witnesses in vv. 5-8, "he appeared to Cephas, then to the twelve. Then he appeared to more than five hundred brothers at one time, most of whom are still alive...Then he appeared to James, then to all the apostles. Last of all...he appeared also to me." Can five hundred brothers suffer hallucination at the same time? All these appearances can not be explained away as some kind of "faith

---

7   John Owen's affirmation is quoted in Donald W. Sweeting & George Sweeting, *How to Finish the Christian Life: Following Jesus in the Second Half*, (Chicago, Ill: Moody Press, 2012), 184.

conviction" rather than the reality that Christ was alive again from the dead.

Paul emphasizes that the resurrection is fundamental to the gospel. The Corinthians originally had been introduced to the Greek idea of the immortality of the soul, and now found it hard to think of the body rising again. Paul makes clear to them what would be the logical conclusion of adopting that position (vv. 12-19). If dead men do not rise, then "not even Christ has been raised." If that is so then the apostles had no message. It is the resurrection that shows that God has set his seal or affirmed his acceptance of the work of the cross as sufficient for sinners – it is God's "Amen" to Christ's "It is finished!" Paul tells it like it is: if Christ is not risen, the gospel message is a sham, "our preaching is in vain." The apostles are deceivers, their faith is "futile" or useless, and those who have already "fallen asleep in Christ have perished" vv.16-18. But Paul affirms "in fact Christ had been raised from the dead" as the witnesses have testified and also, which brings us real hope, he was simply "the firstfruits" (v.20) of the final harvest – Christians will also be raised and the living changed when Christ comes. Having established the fact, he went on to deal with:

THE NATURE OF THE RESURRECTION

To those who would question how a body, which had clearly disintegrated, could ever rise, Paul reminds them of the miracle which happens after the farmer sows his wheat or grain. The seed is buried in the ground and seemingly decays, but it is then raised up with a new and more glorious body! "What you sow is not the body that is to be," (v.37). Again, there are different kinds of bodies as the "heavenly bodies," the sun, moon planets etc. each having their own particular "glory," (v.41). So as God willed to give us bodies fitted for our life on earth, he will give us bodies fitted for our heavenly existence. "So it is with the resurrection of the dead. What is sown is perishable; what is raised is imperishable. It is sown in dishonour (death has defeated it);

it is raised in glory. It is sown in weakness; it is raised in power. It is sown a natural body; it is raised a spiritual body," vv. 42-44. We will have a body, which is incorruptible, glorious – compare a seed to the flower; a body powerful, fitted to spiritual existence. We will be changed. In v.53 Paul explains that this change is essential because man's present condition (one of corruption and mortality) is totally incompatible with life in the hereafter.

THE MOMENT OF THE RESURRECTION
Paul writes, "Behold! I tell you a mystery," v.51. A mystery is not just something mysterious, but something previously hidden which is now being revealed by God. In v.50 Paul has stated the fact that we cannot enter the heavenly world or heavenly mode of existence as we are. We must be changed! He explains how this will happen.

"We shall not all sleep," (v.51). Sleep is a very precious way of referring to death. The bodies of believers are just sleeping for a little while. That is what death really is. The body, but not the spirit,[8] sleeps. I remember once conducting the funeral of a Reserve Policeman. At Tommy's funeral there was a police escort; other policemen stopped the traffic on the route. When a believer dies they have an escort; Luke 16:22, reveals that Lazarus was "carried by the angels" as his body slept.

But some will not even need to sleep or die. As we have noted the perishable body, whether dead or alive, cannot inherit the imperishable life of the future. Paul now affirms "We shall all be changed." This is not a long drawn out affair but will happen "in a moment" (v.52) – the word is atomos, that which cannot be cut or divided – so the shortest possible moment of time, or "in the twinkling of an eye." In a split second.

The last trumpet will sound announcing the arrival of the end events. The trumpet sounding and the dead being raised reminds us of 1Thess. 4:13f. Paul does not want us to be "uninformed...about

---

[8] Cf. e.g., Rev. 6:9 which reveals 'the souls of those who have been slain" who "cried out..."

those who are asleep." He explains again there that Christ's resurrection is the assurance of the resurrection of his people. "Even so, through Jesus, God will bring with him those who have fallen asleep," (v.14). When Christ descends from heaven (actually! bodily!) with "a cry of command, with the voice of the Archangel and with the sound of the trumpet of God" (v.16) the dead in Christ will rise and our bodies will be transformed so we can be "caught up together with them" (v.17) - we will meet first our loved ones and then we meet the Lord! In v.17 again Paul assures us "so we will always be with the Lord." Of course, we have to be with the Lord now (in a saving relationship with him), if we are going to be with him then.

Here in 1 Cor. 15 what Paul is emphasizing are the results of the second coming – resurrection – transformation - the abolition of death itself. "The last enemy," v.26, will be destroyed. We will overcome death. Note the "when" and the "then" of v.54. We will be triumphant over death, but it is still future – when Christ comes. "When the perishable" or "the corruptible" i.e., those believers whose bodies have been corrupting/decaying in the grave, put on the imperishable; also "the mortal" i.e., each one of us still in the body, have put on "immortality," then the words of Isaiah 25:8 will be fulfilled, "He will swallow up death forever." Death is overcome at the second coming of Christ.

In vv.55-56 Paul pictures the experience of death with reference to the sting of serpents or bees. But the sting is not so much in death as in sin, which causes death. Paul has already referred to their sins in vv. 3, 17 and it is this sin which brings death. He also writes of the law "the power of sin is the law," (v.56). The law is what shows to men God's standard, and so reveals to them the depths of their depravity and rebellion against God. So the law is what condemns us and is the "strength of sin", since it provokes a resistance within us, or as Rom. 7:7-8 made clear, "sin, seizing an opportunity through the commandment, produced in me all kinds of covetousness." But through what Christ has done, or the cross of Christ, sin and the condemnation of the law have both been dealt with, as also death has, for we are forgiven and receive eternal life. Death cannot hold us. Death is an enemy but as we noted in v.26, it will be destroyed. There is victory for the Christian, but it is only through what Christ has done for us. So there is no need to be afraid of death. We noted how Paul can state elsewhere, death is "gain" and being with Christ is "far better," Phil. 1:21-23. So, for the child of God death need not be feared. David in Psa. 23:4 affirms, "Even though I walk through the valley of the shadow of death, I will fear no evil, for you are with me." For the one who has turned from sin to Christ, it is not "the valley of death" but "the valley of the shadow of death." The saviour by his death for us has in effect "abolished death and brought life and immortality to light through the gospel," (2 Tim. 1:10). Finally, we should note:

THE CONSEQUENCES OF THE RESURRECTION.

In v. 58 Paul exhorts us to "be steadfast, immovable." With regard to those who have died in Christ, we have hope i.e., certainty. As we saw in 2 Cor. 5:8 they are "at home with the Lord." Also Christ's resurrection is the guarantee of theirs. We grieve, but we know that Christ is coming and those who sleep will be raised. We ought not to be moved away from our chosen path, purpose or commitment.

We are to be "always abounding in the work of the Lord." Always – not in fits and starts. Always "abounding" in the work of the Lord. Let us not be so overcome by our loss, that we remove ourselves from involvement in the church, or the work of the kingdom, but seek to fill our lives with service for him. Paul speaks of our labour to the point of fatigue. Do we know anything about it? All will not be in vain but rewarded. Are we living with eternity's values in view?

CHAPTER SIX

Hope in Seasons of Fear

Isaiah 41:1-9 Are we afraid?

W E NEED NEVER be afraid with his promise "Fear not, for I am with you..." v.10. Summer, winter, springtime, harvest, seasons bring change yet through all the changing scenes of time we know "Great Is His Faithfulness." The emphasis in these chapters (41-44) is on the uniqueness of God compared to the gods of the heathen. The beginning of this present chapter is like a court scene with God addressing first the nations. People must be made to realize that he is the true God, He is the one who controls world history. He invites the nations to know and experience the blessings that Israel is to know. He is:

THE GOD TO BE FEARED

He had the power to deliver Judah from her bondage in Babylon. He also had the will − in fact he desired to bring salvation to the whole world. Note the message of the opening verses.

In v. 1 God addresses the "coastlands," the farthest reaches of the Gentile world, "the ends of the earth," (v.5). He is summoning them to be silent and asking them to listen to him. If they would heed him they too would gain new strength as he had promised his people (40:31; 41:1).

Verse 2 is where God asserts his sovereignty. He was calling and raising up a conqueror. He "stirred up one from the east whom victory meets at every step," (v.2). He would defeat nations and overcome kings, "he tramples kings underfoot"; they are like "driven stubble" blown away, as swiftly as one blows away chaff. This overcomer, later identified as Cyrus (44:28; 45:1), would be able to travel safely over previously unused routes, "by paths his feet have not trod," (v.3).

In v.4f God commands the nations to hear. He affirms that he is the Lord, the one who is in control of history for he is "the first, and with the last." He is sovereign, a God to be feared.

THE NATIONS WHO FEAR

In vv. 5-6 it is revealed that in hearing of his great power, the nations tremble in fear and try to encourage one another. "Everyone helps his neighbor and says to his brother, 'Be strong!'"

Sadly, v. 7 shows us that they proceed to build idols, rather than seeking the Lord. The idol takes a lot of work and needs to pass the inspection of a common labourer! "They strengthen it with nails so that it cannot be moved." The sad fact was that they did not turn to the Lord himself.

God now assures his people in v. 8, "But you, Israel, my servant, Jacob, whom I have chosen, the offspring of Abraham, my friend." He tells them that they need not be afraid. Actually, vv.8-9 is the introduction of what God had to say to his people and v.10 is the real assurance from him. We can apply it to ourselves at this time.

ISRAEL SHOULD NOT FEAR

In vv.8-10 the Lord now speaks to his own people. They were chosen for special blessing. He had brought them from the remotest parts of the earth, "called from its farthest corners" – Abraham from Ur and Jacob from Haran. Why should they worry about being in Babylon? God could recover them from there. This great God was with them and his power was available for them to trust in. To Israel he said, "I have chosen you and not cast you off," (v.10).

HE GIVES THEM A COMMAND

They must not fear or, as he also adds, "be not dismayed" or "do not gaze about in anxiety". The idea is of looking about in all directions to see if there is anything that can harm them or where they can find a place of safety. We think of the mighty power of Babylon.

Are we afraid? One can see national changes, world changes, climate changes. Many are afraid. Think of man's capacity to destroy himself. Luke 21:26 speaks of "people fainting with fear and with foreboding of what is coming on the world." The lack of security can be difficult to handle. You may have particular problems which make you afraid. You may see the threatening clouds in your sky, or on the horizon, or the dark shadows which fall across your path. Yet here we have his command, "Be not afraid."

HE BRINGS THEM HIS COMFORT

"fear not, for I am with you." The text emphasises the promise of his divine presence and help, "with you am I." Why should they fear for their God was with them in all his sufficiency?

"I am your God." Greater resources than this they could not have. His personal commitment is here.

"I will strengthen you, I will help you, I will uphold you with my righteous right hand." All they needed to meet the threats, the severe trials, the problems of temptation they had to bear, is promised. The word for "right hand" signifies the power and might of God. The very waters at creation were measured "in the hollow of his hand," (Isa. 40:12). That same hand can uphold and sustain you!

HE EMPHASISES HIS COMMITMENT

"I will strengthen...I will help you...I will uphold you." This chapter is the great "I will" chapter - 14 times the words appear. These are the first three. When God says "I will" it is said with all the authority of omnipotence.

Can we take him at his word? Trust him?

To Summarise, Israel had A TRINITY OF PROBLEMS; fear; dismay; weakness in the face of great trials. But there was A TRINITY

OF POWER; God was "with" them; he was their God; he was all-sufficient to strengthen, help, uphold. So he gave them A TRINITY OF PROMISES; "I will...I will...I will." In Tit. 1:2 Paul assures us that he is the God who "never lies"; also Joshua 21:45 testifies that as far as the promises made to Israel were concerned, "Not one word of all the good promises that the LORD had made to the house of Israel had failed; all came to pass." His promises to us are just as certain and so we have hope in seasons of fear. Lift your eyes to him and the shadows will be behind you.

CHAPTER SEVEN

Hope Even To Your Old Age

Isa. 46:1-13

T HE YEARS SEEM to fly. Life is but a moment in time, so short, so fleeting. As life progresses we begin to think about how we will cope in old age. In God's comfort here to the exiles in Babylon we can find hope.

"God Knows" was a poem composed by Minnie Louise Haskins published in 1912. The popular name given to it was "The Gate of the Year" and it was brought to the King's attention by his wife suggesting he might use it in his 1939 Christmas broadcast to the British Empire. I always remember the late king George's words:

> I said to the man who stood at the gate of the year, give me a light that I may tread safely into the unknown and he replied, "Go out into the darkness and put your hand into the hand of God. That will be better than light and safer than a known way."

Our God is sufficient to undertake and guide – throughout all the future years. Isaiah shows to Israel the wonder of the God they had. In Isaiah 46 he is contrasted with the gods of the Babylonians. The Almighty is so different from these false gods who are not gods at all. Isaiah reminds them, and of course us also, of his greatness. God is first of all:

A GOD WHO WILL CARRY YOU
Bel and Nebo were the two most prominent deities in the Babylonian pantheon. Bel was Babylon's patron deity and is sometimes called Bel-Marduk and Nebo is the son of Bel-Marduk. Nebo was the god of learning and divine interpretation, the object of devotion on the part

of the intellectual world. Belshazzar and Nebuchadnezzar in the book of Daniel were named after them.

First, in v.1 God reveals what will become of their idols when the Persians finally come to take the city (Daniel 5). Bel and Nebo were no doubt set up on high but "Bel bows down; Nebo stoops." They stoop and bow down at the feet of the soldiers, struck down by a devastating blow. The reference "their idols are on beasts and livestock" and they are "burdens on weary beasts" reveal how the animals strain under the heavy load as the cart lurches along and the gods are themselves carried "into captivity," (v.2).

But in contrast we have God's promise in v.3. Rather than being like the gods of Babylon which have to be carried, we have a God who will carry us! "Listen to me" God says as he speaks prophetically to the captives - but it can also be heeded by those who read it. The idols need to be carried but you have been carried from the very beginning – in fact "before your birth" and "carried from the womb."

How true this is also for us. God has carried you all the way, even from before you were born. A mother carries her child, nurtures and cares for her little one while that child is young. For us God's protecting care is promised right up to the end of life – "even to your old age I am he, and to gray hairs I will carry you. I have made, and I will bear; I will carry and will save," (v.4). Even though you are growing old God will not fail you nor forsake you. In Deut. 33:25 he promises, "As your days so shall your strength be."

"Even to your old age" God promises; when you get unfit for business, when overcome by weakness and infirmity, when your family does not have the same care or time for you, he will not forsake you; he will give you his help and still carry you. But he will do more for the exiles and for us his people.

A GOD WHO WILL HEAR YOU

In v.5 God challenges them as to the fact that he is the incomparable God who cannot be represented by some kind of figure. The text deals in vv.6-7 with the folly of those who make idols and then pray to them! The gold or silver is provided for the image and a goldsmith hired. The dead wood is overlaid with the gold and silver and they lift it up upon their shoulders, carry it to its place more like a dead corpse than a living God and there it stands. What can it do? "It cannot move from its place. If one cries to it, it does not answer or save him from his trouble," (v.7). So the idol cannot move a hand or take a step; neither can it hear the cry of those in need; nor can a dead statue answer or save out of any trouble.

In contrast, our God is the living God who can put forth his mighty arm. You can cry to him in your trouble and he will hear you and help you. Psa. 55:22 reminds us, "Cast your burden on the Lord, and he will sustain you; he will never permit the righteous to be moved." So in v.8 God urges them to take heed to his word. "Remember this and stand firm, recall it to mind, you transgressors." They have transgressed in offering devotion to idols; they must call upon the living God. How often we forget to call upon him in the day of trouble. He is also:

A GOD WHO WILL NOT FAIL YOU
In v.9f. God calls upon them to remember their past, the former course of their history. His powerful hand had already been at work in their past experiences. He is such a great God that he can and has purposed the end from the beginning! His counsel "shall stand" and what he has planned will happen; it will not be changed, for he himself has decreed it. He assures them "I will accomplish all my purpose," (v. 10). His plans and promises will not fail.

He affirms in v.11 that what he has already planned, or promised, he will bring to pass - the deliverance of his people from Babylon (170 years ahead from when Isaiah prophesies). The ravenous bird or "bird of prey" - a falcon or eagle - is Cyrus the Persian who will defeat the Babylonians. To those who are "stubborn of heart, you who are far from righteousness" (v.12) he offers deliverance and the gift of righteousness.

All these are assurances that their God will not fail them. What he had purposed and promised he would do. Your God will not fail you even as the years pass. You are in his hand. As we noted, John 10:28 affirms concerning his sheep, "I give them eternal life, and they will never perish, and no one will snatch them out of my hand" – nor the hand of his Father in v.29. Trust him as you step out into the future. Place your hand in the hand of God.

A GOD WHO WILL GRACIOUSLY SAVE YOU

We have noted that there is a word to those who are "stubborn of heart" and are "far from righteousness." The reference is to those who resist God and have no righteousness of their own. The glorious news is that God has brought his own righteousness near. We have not got to seek to obtain salvation or righteousness by our own efforts or good works; salvation is a gift from him alone. God calls it "my righteousness" not our own. In grace he has brought it near and we can obtain it. You can reach God just where you are. Note in closing this chapter we learn of:

THE NEED OF RIGHTEOUSNESS

In v.12 we are "far" from righteousness. Paul can affirm "All have sinned, and fall short of the glory of God," Rom. 3:23; our own righteousness is by comparison to that of God's righteousness like "a polluted garment" Isa. 64:6; the attempt to keep the law only shows up our sinfulness. Rom. 3:20 makes it clear that "For by works of the law no human being will be justified in his sight, since through the law comes knowledge of sin."

THE NATURE OF RIGHTEOUSNESS

God calls it "my" righteousness. If we have "his" then we will be surely accepted. It is in the person of his son. Focusing again on Isaiah, the prophet reveals that when Israel was in Babylon there was not just ONE servant of the LORD but TWO, the political servant mentioned already, Cyrus and also the "suffering" servant bringing near God's righteousness. He is the one prophesied in Isa. 52:13-53:12, the one who would be "wounded for our transgressions," whose soul "makes an offering for guilt," (vv.5, 10).   This "righteous one, my servant" will "make many to be accounted righteousness," for "he shall bear their iniquities," (v. 11). The Lord Jesus Christ is that suffering servant who himself perfectly lived the law, so he could take the place of the guilty and redeem those who broke the law and were condemned by it. When we could do nothing to get right will God and were without hope, God himself in love took the initiative in giving his own son. "But when the fullness of time had come, God sent forth his son...to redeem," Gal. 4:4-5.

THE NEARNESS OF RIGHTEOUSNESS

In this way God "brings near" his righteousness. Have you neglected it or possessed it? Rom. 10:8 reveals that this blessing is not far off for it is in the gospel of good news we preach. "The word is near you, in your mouth and in your heart (that is, the word of faith that we proclaim)." You can reach it – or reach him - where you are. You must turn from your own independence of God, your rebellion, or as Isa. 53:6 puts it "All we like sheep have gone astray; we have turned – every one – to his own way." Turn from taking your own way, believe the good news of what God has done in sending his own son to pay the price for sinners and in faith put your trust in him.

So you can be right with him and he can be there for you all of your life, every step, every day.

CHAPTER EIGHT

Hope When You Feel Like Running Away

Psalm 55:1-23

HAVE YOU EVER felt like running away? It is difficult when things get on top of you and you are unable to cope. You can find yourself in stressful situations. The threatening shadows of life close in around you. Listen to the words of David in v.6, "Oh that I had wings like a dove! I would fly away and be at rest." David wanted to run away or to put it more accurately – to fly away. The Psalm reveals that rebellion was abroad, which most connect with the rebellion led by Absalom his son. This was the time of the treachery of Ahithophel when as a trusted counsellor he betrayed the king, 2 Samuel 16-17. The whole city was against him, as he states in vv. 9-11; "for I see violence and strife in the city. Day and night they go around it on its walls." David was perhaps on the roof of the palace or on the highest hill of Jerusalem. It has been suggested that perhaps a dove alights and begins to coo. As she sees David the startled bird takes flight and soars up into the distant sky. Did David, observing this, long to do the same? When things get to the point of crisis, often people react in this way. Remember also Jeremiah 9:2 where the weeping prophet moans, "Oh that I had in the desert a travelers' lodging place, that I might leave my people and go away from them."

Henry Wadsworth Longfellow[9] was an American poet who expressed the same yearning in a poem called "The Bridge."

---

9   H.W. Longfellow's poem in *The New Anthology of American Poetry: Traditions and Revolutions, Beginnings to 1900,* eds., S. G. Axelrod, C. Roman, T. Travisano, (New Brunswick, New Jersey and London: Rutgers University Press, 2003), 234.

How often, oh how often
In the days that had gone by,
I had stood on the bridge at midnight,
And gazed on the wave and sky.

How often, oh how often,
I had wished that the ebbing tide,
Would bear me away on its bosom,
O'er the ocean wild and wide.

For my heart was hot and restless,
And my life was full of care,
And the burden laid upon me,
Seemed greater than I could bear."

David had been a great warrior, king, psalmist, a man after God's own heart. But he wanted to fly away from it all. What was it that brought David to this place?

DAVID'S MANY PROBLEMS

1. He was faced with bitterness, hostility, slander and threats from his enemies causing him to be afraid. We see this in vv.1-11.

   He cries to God not to forget about him but to come to help him. In his distress he groans and prays, "because of the noise of the enemy, because of the oppression of the wicked. For they drop trouble upon me, and in anger they bear a grudge against me," v.3. The mental distress is revealed in v.4 where David reveals "My heart is in anguish within me; the terrors of death have fallen upon me" and in v.5 "fear and trembling" come upon him and he is "overwhelmed" with horror.

   Have you known something of this bitterness, hostility and false accusation? The world and the flesh and the devil are against you.

David did not know what would happen next or when the worst would come. He wanted to fly away (vv. 6-8). Perhaps you share the same feelings because things are not easy for you. There are darkening skies and deep shadows.

2. He wanted to flee from the torture of a broken heart. The leader of the rebellion was Absalom, his own son. Think of the grief and heartache that can be caused in family situations. The worry they can bring into your life.

3. He wanted to get away from a tormenting memory, i.e., how he had sinned in 2 Sam.11:1-26. He found it impossible to keep the thoughts of his transgressions out of his memory. He would be tortured by what he had done to Bathsheba and what he did to her husband! The prophet had warned the king that "the sword shall never depart from your house" (2 Sam. 12:10). He was thinking that there was no one to blame but himself.

4. He wanted to get away from an atmosphere which was poisoned by ingratitude and lack of appreciation. His best friend had become unfaithful to him. "For it is not an enemy who taunts me – then I could bear it; it is not an adversary who deals insolently with me – then I could hide from him. But it is you, a man, my equal, my companion, my familiar friend. We used to take sweet counsel together; within God's house we walked in the throng," vv.12-14. He now felt abandoned, betrayed and forsaken.

5. He was faced with a task to which he felt himself unequal. Rebellion was abroad; the weight of years was upon him; he was tired and was tempted to throw down the weight of responsibility. He could not do it any more.

DAVID'S READY ANSWER

He wanted to fly away, to go to the wilderness, vv.6-7. That was his old home. It was there that he had spent his childhood and early youth. He had watched the sheep and had spent carefree years before he wore the crown that had now brought to him all the heartache. He wanted away from the storms and trials of life, "I would hurry to find a shelter from the raging wind and tempest," v.8.

Have we not all experienced the same feelings at times? I could also have run away from situations in ministry and gone back to Ballyhalbert, Co. Down where I spent the happy days of my childhood. I told myself that I would go back to where as a boy I swam in the sea, carefree days, where I fished, played, rode my bike, gathered mushrooms in the aerodrome. But this was not the answer. Nor is it for you. We can never go back, only forward.

DAVID'S ONLY SOLUTION

Running away would not help for he would take his troubles with him. The attainment of rest does not depend upon flight. Nor was it the remedy for his ills. His only remedy was in God. We see this in v.16. "But I (this is emphatic) call to God and the LORD will save me." Evening and morning and at noonday he cried to God; he was leaning continually upon him (v.17); he will be delivered. God will give him peace. David can testify, "He redeems my soul in safety from the battle that I wage," (v.18). From v.22 we see that what was needed was not a new physical atmosphere but a new spiritual atmosphere. Not the wings of a dove, but rather the everlasting arms into which he could cast his great burden. "Cast your burden on the LORD, and he will sustain you; he will never permit the righteous to be moved." Therefore hope is not in flight but in God; prayer and faith in God in whom he must trust, v. 23.

Notice the importance of v.22. There is a LOAD here; your "burden". It may be health, relationships or distressing circumstances or trial. There is One, our LORD here; he knows, he has allowed this situation; but he is still in control – like Job's situation when the Lord said to Satan concerning him in Job 2:6, "Behold, he is in your hand: only spare his life." There is a LOOSING here; "cast your burden upon" and to "cast" it you must let it go and leave it with him. We often want to bring it away with us again! There is a LIFTING UP here, for it is promised "He will sustain you." What a promise!

Spurgeon[10] in *The Treasury of David*, puts it like this:

> Thy burden, or what thy God lays upon thee, lay thou it upon the Lord. His wisdom casts it on thee, it is thy wisdom to cast it upon him…He gives thee thy portion of suffering, accept it with cheerful resignation and then take it back to him by thine assured confidence. He will sustain thee.

Do not fly from him; but fly to him. He is the GLORY BEARER who will return in power and "bear royal honor," (Zech. 6:13); he is the SIN BEARER (1 Peter 2:24) who "bore our sins" in his own body to make it possible for his people who turn to him and put their trust alone in him to share his glory in that great day. But until then he has not left you to struggle through alone; until that day he is your BURDEN BEARER (Psa. 55:22). When you feel like running and there is no place to run, run to him. As we emphasised earlier, when you turn your eyes toward him the shadows will be behind you.

---

[10] C. H, Spurgeon, *The Treasury of David*, Vol. 1 (Edinburgh: B. McCall Barbour, 1977), 451.

CHAPTER NINE

Hope When You Have Sadly Failed

SIMON PETER IS an example of a man who gives us hope when we have failed. It is precious to know that God is the God of the second chance.

In every list of the disciples Peter is named first. In Mark 1:29-30 we discover that Peter was married and lived at Capernaum; we read of his mother-in-law. His home was there – here we also read of "the house of Simon and Andrew" who was his brother. Note that he is called Simon when he first appears on the scene. It is his own name – Matthew calls him 'Simon, who is called Peter," Matt. 4:18; 10:2 and he is called it on domestic occasions.   He has a fishing boat, Mark1:29-30; Luke 5:3, 10. There is so much in the NT about him. I want to focus on a phrase about "looking" at Peter. It will help us to see the whole story of his sad failure and loving restoration. We learn from Peter that there is hope.

In John 1:35-51 we read of the first meeting of Jesus with his disciples. In vv. 35-42 we are introduced to two of John the Baptist's disciples, one called Andrew. They leave John and "follow" the one identified as "the Lamb of God," Jesus himself.   Of Andrew we read "he first found his own brother Simon," (v.41). Was this the first thing he did when he came to believe? Or was Peter just the first one he found? Both are true. He goes on in John's Gospel to "find" others for Jesus – in 6:9 a boy with five barley loaves and two fish and in 12:20-22 Greeks who have come to Jerusalem to worship at the feast. Andrew wanted others to find Jesus too; it was a priority in his life. When you yourself find Jesus you are at once qualified - and obligated - to tell what you know. Here we learn of Andrew, "He brought him to Jesus," (v.42). Now the important phrase.

John 1:42 "Jesus looked at him."

Hendriksen[11] tells us that this statement implies a close penetrating look. Moffatt translates, "he gazed at him"; Knox has "looked at him fixedly" and finally, JB Phillips suggests, "looked steadily at him". This statement means that Jesus fixed his eyes on Simon; he gazed at him. Jesus both looked at and into him as only God could do. Here we have in v.42 Jesus' response. "So you are Simon the son of John? You shall be called Cephas" (which means Peter). His new name Cephas is the Aramaic; Peter is the Greek. Both carry the meaning of "rock." It is also stressed by the other Gospel writers that Jesus gave him this name, Mark 3:16; Luke 4:38.

Why change his name from Simon? He was not what God meant him to be, alienated from God. Changing his name was not for novelty, but reflects what God wanted him to be. God wants to change your relationship with him. Are you without him? Eph. 2:12 reminds us that as we begin in life, we have "no hope" no matter what we could ever do and are "without God in the world."

Jesus had a place for Peter in God's plan. God's purpose was to save him, to change him and to use him. What about you? Have you ever thought that God has plans for you and your life? He has the power to change him from Simon, son of John to Cephas, Peter, stone or rock-like. God could bring about a life-giving change in Peter and in us.

He could change his vocation. Matt.4:18-19 informs us that "While walking by the Sea of Galilee, he (Jesus) saw two brothers, Simon (who is called Peter) and Andrew his brother, casting a net into the sea, for they were fishermen. And he said to them, 'Follow me, and I will make you fishers of men.'" Peter had not only his own boat but partners in the fishing business, Luke 5:3, 7, 10 mentions "James and John, sons

---

[11] W. Hendriksen, *The Gospel of John*, (London: Banner of Truth Trust, 1964), 106.

of Zebedee, who were partners with Simon." But Jesus had a far greater work for him to do. There is no greater work that winning souls and seeking to shepherd God's people.

God could also change his view of Jesus. In John 6:68 Simon Peter can confess, "Lord, to whom shall we go? You have the words of eternal life." Again, in Matt. 16:16 he can say, "You are the Christ, the Son of the living God." What is your view of Jesus? Have you grasped that he is the one who can give you life; the one who needs to be your king? God enabled Peter to venture upon Jesus. In Matt. 14:22-34, in the storm on the lake the boat was "beaten by the waves." Jesus comes to them walking on the water, and says "Take heart; it is I. Do not be afraid," (v. 27). Peter answers, "Lord, if it is you, command me to come to you on the water." Jesus said "Come," (v. 28-29). What a moment when Peter got out of the boat and walked on the water! We are then told, "But when he saw the wind, he was afraid, and beginning to sink he cried out, 'Lord save me,'" (v.30). Jesus immediately reached out his hand and took hold of him, saying, "O you of little faith, why did you doubt?" What a lesson for Peter and the rest – that in the future in the many storms his people would pass through he would be there and was sufficient. The aim initially was to get Peter to trust him, to reach out the hand of faith to Jesus. We need to learn this lesson as well.

Peter also had to change his vision of Jesus and his purpose. In Mark 8:29-33 in a Gospel written by Mark but here really Peter's memoirs, after Peter confesses Jesus as the Christ, Jesus reveals his future sufferings. "the Son of Man must suffer many things and be rejected by the elders and the chief priests and be killed, and after three days rise again," (8:31). We are told that "Peter took him aside and began to rebuke him. But turning and seeing his disciples, he rebuked Peter and said, 'Get behind me, Satan! For you are not setting your mind on the things of God, but on the things of man'," (8:32-33). From Jesus he is learning that the cross is the will and purpose of God for his Master.

So Peter experienced many changes; but most of all, Jesus wanted to change HIM. He also must die to self, Mark 8:34. "Denying oneself" means not just to disown one's sins but one's self, to turn away from the idolatry of self-centredness to "follow" him. Here again Peter is the picture of a typical disciple. But more was to come.

Mark 14:66-67. "she looked at him"

In this passage we read of one of the servant girls of the high priest who saw Peter warming himself at the fire in the courtyard, when he had followed Jesus there "at a distance," (v.54). First she looked at him and then she began to frown, to express puzzlement. "You also were with the Nazarene, Jesus." Here he denies him, v.68, and again, v.70, and again, to the "bystanders" v.71 "he began to invoke a curse on himself and to swear." Three times, before the cock would crow, at daybreak Peter had denied his Lord.

Peter, in v.54 had access because of John the disciple of Jesus, John 18:13, 16. He sat down with palace servants and temple guards as they warmed themselves. Peter could publically state in Matt. 26:33-35 with regard to himself and the other disciples, "Though they all fall away because of you, I will never fall away...Even if I must die with you, I will not deny you!" He also could jump to Jesus' defence in the garden – cutting off the high priest's servant's ear - but he still had not learned that he cannot stand alone - even before a slip of a girl he denies his Lord. We must remember 1 Cor. 10:12 "Let anyone who thinks that he stands take heed lest he fall." We need to live close to the Lord to be safe. Why did he deny Jesus?

(1) Peter was impetuous. He speaks before he thinks. For example, in Matt. 16:22, (parallel to Mark 8:32) when Jesus reveals how he must go to Jerusalem, suffer and die, Peter rebukes him, "Far be it from you Lord! This shall never happen to you." Again, in Mark 9:5-6, when Jesus is on the Mount of Transfiguration with Moses

and Elijah, Peter suggests, "Rabbi, it is good that we are here. Let us make three tents, one for you and one for Moses and one for Elijah." Finally, in John 13:6-9, when Jesus will take the basin and towel and begin to wash the disciples' feet, he protests, "You shall never wash my feet!" So there were times when Peter spoke the first thing which came into his head when he not yet grasped the issues at stake or the significance of what Jesus was doing. He needed to learn as so often do we. People sometimes get up and say things which would have been better left unsaid. Satan can destroy a work by hastily spoken words. See James 1:19-20, "Know this my beloved brothers: let every person be quick to hear, slow to speak, slow to anger. For the anger of man does not produce the righteousness of God," i.e., the righteous example God is looking for in his people. Again, Peter could also act at times before thinking, e.g., taking up the sword and attacking the high priest's servant, as has been mentioned, John 18:10-11; going back to the fishing, 21:3. We must often learn to wait for the guidance of God. This is so important, or the devil will get an advantage over us.

(2)   Peter was marked by a rash self-confidence, seeing himself as better than others, Mark 14:27-31 – Peter can state, "though they all...I will not." Yet shortly after, he had denied his Lord three times; to a young girl, vv.66-67; a second time, v.69; and to some bystanders, v.70. We cannot stand alone, for in John 15:5 Jesus reminds us, "apart from me you can do nothing." But Peter had not yet learned this. We remember Phil. 4:13, "I can do all things through him who strengthens me."

(3)   There had been a failure to watch and pray in the garden, In Mark 14:37-40, in Gethsemane Jesus finds the disciples asleep and challenges first Peter, "Simon, are you asleep? Could you not watch one hour? Watch and pray that you may not enter into temptation." No less than three times it was to be repeated. This is almost always where failure first starts, failure which can lead to

moral or spiritual disaster. Not being on your guard or keeping in touch with God, a failure to pray. Our absence at the hour of prayer is where it all can begin.

(4) Peter did not heed the Lord's warnings to him. In Luke 22:31-34 Jesus warned Peter. He used his old name "Simon," for he had and would in the events that were to unfold allow self to rule in his life. He would not really listen. Jesus reveals that Satan had designs on them all – "Simon, Simon, behold, Satan demanded to have you, that he might sift you like wheat, but I have prayed for you that your faith may not fail." The first use of "you" is plural, the second, singular. Satan wanted to sift them all, to only leave the chaff for Christ. But we will note that the opposite purpose is why God allows it.

Note Satan has to ask to do this. The precious situation is that you are the Lord's and it is only as God allows can Satan attack us. As we saw earlier in Job 1:10-12 God could say to Satan concerning his servant Job, "Behold, all that he has is in your hand. Only against him do not stretch out your hand." Again, in chapter 2:4-6, God could once more limit Satan, "Behold, he is in your hand; only spare his life." If God allows you to be given into Satan's hands, the devil's purpose and God's purpose will be very different. No doubt Satan will be attempting to destroy you, but as far as God is concerned he will be planning that good will result from the situation; that as you are severely tested you will in the end by faith endure and advance in godliness. God knows the end from the beginning, he knows what he is doing; he was in charge as far as Job was concerned. So also with us.

Do we always take the warnings of Scripture seriously? Peter failed to do this here for his response was as was mentioned above, "Lord, I am ready to go with you both to prison and to death." Jesus reveals the reality of what was about to happen, "I tell you Peter, the rooster will not crow this day, until you deny three times that you know me," (Luke 22:33-34). But he did not heed the warnings. Often we are just the same.

(5) He did not confess Jesus but hid his light at the charcoal fire, John 18:18. Jerusalem was 3,000 feet above sea level, so the night would be cold. The servants and officers of the High Priest had made a fire which would be lit for warmth and for light and Peter was recognised in the firelight. We see him lingering at the fire in the courtyard, in the company of his enemies with his light hidden. He was ashamed of Jesus. You must learn to let your light shine.

(6) He did not walk by faith. He did not see the purpose of God in the death of Jesus, as we saw in Mark 8:32-33. When we do not walk by faith and endeavour to see the purpose of God, we can resort to carnal methods and even intrigue to get our own way – in John 18:10-11 as we saw, Peter cut off the ear of the servant of the High Priest! But this was not the end of the story - note again the words of Jesus in Luke 22:32, "when you have turned again." Praise God this is possible as we will see shortly. God is the God of the second chance. Observe how the Lord dealt with Peter. Here there is a third look.

Luke 22:61 "And the Lord turned and looked at Peter."

Before he had even finished his denial it is recorded in Luke 22:60 "And immediately, while he was still speaking, the rooster crowed." At that precise moment we have the "look" from Jesus. What a look that must have been. Through it we are told Peter "went out and wept bitterly," (22:62). Oh the pain of failure, of denial, of being overcome in the moment of temptation! How often this has happened down the centuries. One feels that there is no hope, the shadows close around us; all is lost and there is no way back. But here we learn that there is. When Jesus was raised from the dead in Mark 16:1-7 the women came to the tomb. To their amazement the huge stone had been rolled away from the entrance and an angel announced that their Master was alive again from the dead. The message for them was "Go, tell his disciples and Peter that he is going before you to Galilee. There you will see him, just as he told you." What a message for a hurting conscience and a grieving heart over his sin! "Tell his disciples, but do not forget to tell Peter. Do not leave Peter out." God still wanted Peter and we know that somewhere, sometime on that special resurrection day the Lord met Peter! In 1 Cor15:5 Paul as he records the many witnesses to the resurrection of Jesus reveals that "he appeared to Cephas, then to the twelve." What a moment it must have been when Jesus met him that day. Finally we have John 21:15-17, eight days after his first appearance.

Peter with six of Jesus' disciples goes fishing. He is back in "the" boat (21:3), his old boat; but that night they caught nothing. What a moment when we are told "Jesus stood on the shore," (v.4). The Lord would not let Peter and the others go. When Christ directed their fishing there was a huge catch (v.11). But the Lord had a greater ministry planned for Peter – rather than 153 large fish from the Sea of Tiberius, as "a fisher of men" a restored and forgiven Peter would be used to reach 3,000 souls on the day of Pentecost and 5,000 at the Beautiful Gate of the temple, (Acts 2:41; 4:4). Here in John 21:15-19 Jesus challenges Peter about his former failure and sin. Peter finds himself at another charcoal fire like 18:18, but here the Lord is the host with bread and the fish they could not obtain during the long night already provided! In vv. 15-19 like the three denials, Jesus challenges Peter using his former name "Simon, son of John," (John 1:42; 21:15, 16, 17) about his love for him. His Master is looking for *agapē* love, the strongest/deepest word for love. His disciple will not go any further than profess what most commentators will understand in this particular context as his *phileō*, lesser love. Yet this is surely significant. Peter will no longer in any way boast of his great loyalty – or great love for Christ. He has learned at the earlier charcoal fire that he is weak, that he cannot stand by himself – lessons which were vital for any leadership role in the future church of God. Jesus takes him again as at the beginning in John 1, this time in what is almost a re-commission, saying "follow me," (21:19).

Have you failed miserably? Are you deeply troubled about how you have sinned or succumbed unexpectedly in temptation or made the wrong choice in situations where your judgment was required? You have questioned yourself again and again lamenting over how you ever could have done what you did. Do not let the dark shadow of failure engulf you. Here is hope. Jesus still has a place for you in his work. You can begin again. Confess and forsake your sin, give yourself unreservedly to him. Follow him.

Here is an example of one who was able to begin again. Note the contrasts now with the restored disciple compared to his former actions and understanding. In Acts Peter takes the lead – but leaves the choice to God, in the replacement of Judas Iscariot, (1:16-26); he has faith in the fulfilment of the OT prophesies, "Brothers, the Scripture had to be fulfilled, which the Holy Spirit spoke beforehand by the mouth of David concerning Judas…For it is written in the Book of Psalms, 'May his camp become desolate, and let there be no one to dwell in it'; and 'Let another take his office,'" (1:16-20); he accepts his vocation as a dedicated witness to the risen Christ, "I have no silver and gold, but what I do have I give to you," (3:4-6); he acknowledges the plan of God in Jesus' death, "this Jesus, delivered up according to the definite plan and foreknowledge of God, you crucified and killed by the hands of lawless men," (2:23); we see his use of "the keys of the kingdom" - remember Jesus' plan for Peter as the saviour would build his church, "I will give you the keys of the kingdom of heaven," (Matt. 16:19). This was fulfilled both in Acts 2 and Acts 10 – through his preaching, as the door was opened[12] by repentance and faith to Jews and Gentiles.

---

[12]   Note when Paul and Barnabas returned from their first missionary journey they reported what God had done to the church in Antioch in these terms, "they declared all that God had done with them, and how he had opened a door of faith to the Gentiles," Acts 14:27.

In contrast to his past failure, he no longer denies Jesus but is bold before the whole Sanhedrin and is filled with the Holy Spirit, (4:8-13); in the case of Ananias and Sapphira who "sold a piece of property, and with his wife's knowledge he kept back for himself some of the proceeds and brought only a part of it" as if it was the whole. Peter is concerned now about the truth; they must not lie or be deceivers, (5:1-11); he is dependant now on the Lord in the raising of Dorcas from the dead, as he "put them all outside, and knelt down and prayed…" in 9:36-42; he is serene and in faith can sleep in the face of death, when Herod, having killed James seized Peter, "put him in prison, delivering him over to four squads of soldiers to guard him, intending after the Passover to bring him out to the people," (12:4). When Herod was about to kill him, "on that very night, Peter was sleeping between two soldiers, bound with two chains" – sleeping because Jesus had revealed to him at the Sea of Tiberius in John 21:18 "when you are old, you will stretch out your hands, and another will dress you and carry you where you do not want to go." Peter knew that this was not the time! Finally, his wisdom was clear in his contribution at the Jerusalem council, (15:7-11). When some present are asking for the circumcision of Gentile converts and their submission to aspects of the law, Peter can direct them, "Why are you putting God to the test by placing a yoke on the neck of the disciples that neither our fathers nor we have been able to bear? But we believe that we will be saved through the grace of the Lord Jesus, just as they will," (15:10-11).

There is hope for those who have failed and failed miserably. God can take you up again. As has been stated, he is the God of the second chance. But even in this we cannot limit him. He can forgive and lift up the penitent; he can restore and recommission.

CHAPTER TEN

Hope When Your Foot Has Almost Slipped

Psalm 73

THERE IS A superscription to this psalm which tells us that it is from Asaph. Or it may have been given to him to be sung. He was one of David's chief musicians who was involved in directing the worship in the temple (cf. 1 Chron. 6:39; 15:16-19; 16:5, 7, 37; 25:1-2).

This psalm is a record of mental struggle. Here are the questionings which the psalmist experienced as he was faced with the prosperity of the wicked and by contrast, the difficult circumstances of the righteous. In v.2 he reveals "But as for me, my feet had almost stumbled, my steps had nearly slipped." In this psalm he really opens his heart; he reveals how he struggled with this problem and it was written to reveal what was in his heart.

The psalm basically could be divided into two parts:

vv.1-15 The Trial of His Faith. He sees the prosperity of the wicked, which troubles him deeply. If God exists, and he is good so that he can reward the righteous, and he is all-powerful, totally in control of his creation, then why is it that in God's world the wicked seem to be doing better than the righteous? It appears that the sinners succeed and the saints suffer.

vv.16-28 The Triumph of His Faith. This only happens when he goes into the sanctuary of God. He can then see things from a different perspective.

As was noted the psalm sets out the Psalmist's mental struggle, what was going on in his heart. We will look at the whole teaching from this perspective. It is first:

THE PSALM OF THE CLEAN HEART v.1

In this opening verse it is affirmed "Truly God is good to Israel, to those who are pure in heart." This of course was written after he had gone through the mental battle into victory overcoming his negative thoughts concerning the wicked and the righteous. Therefore he can begin with this testimony, declaring his own faith in the goodness of God and is really affirming all who like him are obedient and seek to be holy. He is testifying that he himself had a clean heart.

This is what God expects of us, how we should live and the rest of the psalm reveals why. It is his pilgrimage and how he reached this conviction. He had kept his own heart clean and testifies of his holiness of life, "I have…washed my hands in innocence," (v.13). How do we live our lives? Are we keeping our public and inner life holy? Is there a transparency between us and God? Have you a clean heart? What do you allow? We remember the words of David in Psalm 19:14 "Let the words of my mouth and the meditation of my heart be acceptable in your sight, O LORD, my rock and my redeemer." So also Paul in Phil. 4:8 "Finally brothers, whatever is true, whatever is honorable, whatever is just, whatever is pure, whatever is lovely, whatever is commendable, if there is any excellence, if there is anything worthy of praise, think about these things." But see how he arrived there. The psalm is also:

THE PSALM OF THE TROUBLED HEART vv.2-14

He states that his feet had almost slipped and he had nearly lost his footing (v.2). The spiritual stability of the psalmist had been shaken. His faith was mightily challenged. We might say in our own idiom, "he had nearly lost his grip." The cause of the problem again was what was in his heart, he was "envious" (v.3) at "the arrogance" or pride and concerning "the prosperity" (here we have the Hebrew shalom, which is basically the peace, the well-being) of the wicked. Sadly, he was not troubled so much by the sin of the wicked as he was by their success. We must remember that this is not true of all the wicked – that they all prosper and all the righteous suffer material loss. But it is a generalization and how one can see things from just an earthly perspective.

Now in vv.6-12 the psalmist can sing of the lifestyle of the wicked. We can note first:

(1) vv.4-5 Their Physical Well-being. They had no physical weaknesses, their bodies were healthy, "fat and sleek." They were experiencing no trouble, pain, or distress. They seem to get through life with few problems compared with the righteous. They appear to be immune from the trials of life.

(2) vv.6-8 Their Selfish Pride. The psalmist described it as a "necklace" which would be worn in the Ancient Near East as a sign of status (cf. Gen. 41:42, where Pharaoh put a "gold chain" around Joseph's neck and promoted him in Egypt when he had interpreted his dream). The wicked rich clearly lacked compassion. Instead of using their success and status as a means of helping others, they used it as a selfish tool for gaining even further riches, at the expense of the poor. The psalmist had witnessed the callousness or cruelty of the wealthy. He could see that they were not content with what they had but continually schemed to gain more and more. "Their eyes swell out through fatness; their hearts overflow with follies," (v.7). They were actually boasting of how they were successful in oppressing others to bring about an increase of their own wealth and standing. "They scoff and speak with malice; loftily they threaten oppression," (v. 8).

(3) v.9 Their Arrogant Blasphemy. The wicked are so bold that their blasphemy of God knows no limits (note the use of the spatial images of heaven and earth). They elevate themselves to god-like

levels (cf. v.9 "they set their mouths against the heavens," with Isa. 14:13-14, "You said in your heart, I will ascend to heaven; above the stars of God").

(4) vv.10-11 Their Godless Influence. These are difficult verses to interpret. The wicked who prospered appear to influence the people who witnessed their affluence and status so that they also were tempted to turn to adopt their lifestyle and do as they had done. Or they were being oppressed by the wicked. The wicked went so far as to say, "How can God know? Is their knowledge in the Most High?" (v. 11). It was not that they were denying his existence but his awareness of their actions. He must be some kind of local god, limited in his knowledge of their acts and limited in his power.

So in his perception of things at this point he can write "Behold, these are the wicked; always at ease, they increase in riches," (v.12).

It is clear that here the psalmist is revealing his secret thoughts. He had kept himself pure and had lived a holy life. Yet he saw that the wicked prospered as he had set out in vv.4-12. But these thoughts were never shared until after he had reached a change of attitude or mind. You also will often have thoughts when you see how things are. We should note that here he did not share the soul-searching questions of his heart until after he had found the answer to them. So he did not complain, "If I had said, 'I will speak thus,' I would have betrayed the generation of your children," (v.15). Therefore he informs us that he kept his thoughts to himself. He was the one who had been plagued with trouble while the wicked enjoyed the good life. His faith was deeply challenged and his feet had nearly slipped. But the psalm is also:

THE PSALM OF THE STRICKEN HEART vv. 16-25

He became convicted concerning his thoughts. This is because he came to a new perspective of how things really were. What was it that gave him a new or actually the real perspective on how things are? This came about through what he tells us in v.17 "until I went into the sanctuary of God; then I discerned their end." When he was in "the sanctuary" God showed him things as they really were. His heart was now convicted about the things he had thought. He addresses God directly in these verses see e.g., v.15 "If I had said 'I will speak thus,' I would have betrayed the generation of your children," and v.18 "Truly you set them (the wicked) in slippery places; you make them fall to ruin." His private thoughts were a burden to him, "a wearisome task" to understand why (v.16), until he found the answer in the presence of God. "Until I went into the sanctuary of God; then I discerned their end," (v.17).

We are created to glorify God. We are creatures to honour our creator in every way. Remember the words of Daniel to Belshazzar in Daniel 5:22-23 who knew how God had humbled and then lifted up Nebuchadnezzar before him "And you his son, Belshazzar, have not humbled your heart, though you knew all this…but the God in whose hand is your breath, and whose are all your ways, have you not honored." Again, in 2 Tim. 3:1-5 we are given a glimpse of people "in the last days." "For people will be lovers of self, lovers of money, proud, arrogant, abusive, disobedient to their parents, ungrateful, unholy, heartless, unappeasable, slanderous, without self-control, brutal, not loving good, treacherous, reckless, swollen with conceit, lovers of pleasure rather than lovers of God." We all have failed to honour or glorify him, as we noted in Isaiah 53:6, "All we like sheep have gone astray; we have turned – every one – to his own way." Rather than God's way, submitting to him, it is "my way"; we will do what we want, not what God wants, in effect we say, "I will do what I want to do. I will say what I want to say. I will be what I want to be." We dethrone God and put self on the throne of our lives. We only deserve God's wrath for this rebellion. Here in vv.18-20 the psalmist describes with awe the fate of the ungodly. They are exposed to his wrath, "Truly you set them in slippery places; you make them fall to ruin." The "truly" of v. 18

points out how they are stable one moment and then suddenly they fall. How important to consider these things – where we are with God.

The psalmist confessed his sin in v. 22 "I was brutish and ignorant; I was like a beast toward you" – the beast never lifts its eyes toward heaven or is conscious of God! But the truly satisfying life, the life of true riches, is in a relationship with the living God. What a wonder to know and understand what the psalmist expresses concerning the living God. "Nevertheless, I am continually with you; you hold my right hand. You guide me with your counsel, and afterward you will receive me to glory," (vv.23-24). Walking with God, upheld by God, guided by God. He knows that not only is God all-sufficient throughout his whole life, but that he was going home to God at the last. Satisfied in God now in the present; forever with God in the future! In his foolishness he had forgotten this. He had not truly walked with God or had a faith perspective. He confesses his failure to see things as they really were. With God he has all that he needs; having the Lord in the centre of his life satisfies his whole longings. Now also the psalm is:

THE PSALM OF THE STRENGTHENED HEART vv.26-27

Of course this strength came from God himself. The psalmist continues his witness by reaffirming his allegiance to his God. His feet had almost slipped but he now testifies that God is "the strength of my heart and my portion forever." He stresses that those who are FAR from God, those unfaithful to God will perish. But for him, the reality of God fills his whole life. He has the presence and help of the one who is all-sufficient for the present and the future. But there is more for the psalm is finally:

THE PSALM OF THE OVERFLOWING HEART v.28

Rather than being FAR from him the psalmist confesses the joy of being NEAR to him. "I have made the Lord LORD my refuge." Those who come to him, trust in him and let him be their refuge are truly blessed. So he turns from revealing his troubled thoughts in the past to actually confessing and proclaiming God's wonderful works! His heart is now full to overflowing; his only longing is that men may also come to know the living God and his wonderful works.

If you are still "far" from God, accountable to him and perishing, remember the glorious good news of the Scripture which affirms that "God so loved the world that gave his only Son, that whoever believes in him should not perish but have eternal life," John 3:16. Rom. 3:25 reveals that God in love took the initiative for helpless and hopeless sinners who could never get right with God, and "put forward as a propitiation by his blood" his own Son. It is the death of Christ for us that means the removal of wrath from all who repent of their sin and independence and look to him alone for acceptance – you can also come near to God!

CHAPTER ELEVEN

Hope in the Darkest Hour

I Kings 19:1-21

DEEP SHADOWS AND dark days come at this moment in the life of the prophet Elijah. He feels his whole situation deeply. To appreciate his circumstances note how that when Ahab the king tells Jezebel all that Elijah had done in killing the prophets of Baal, she sent a messenger to the prophet. "So may the gods do to me and more also, if I do not make your life as the life of one of them by this time tomorrow," (v.2). What was Elijah's response? "Then he was afraid, and he arose and ran for his life," (v.3).

It is important to look at the contrast between chapter 18 and 19. In 18:46 Elijah RUNS TO the city of Jezreel as "the hand of the Lord" enabled him. But in 19:2-3 he RUNS FROM Jezreel and from Jezebel's hand. In chapter 18 Elijah is strong in faith, the encourager of his nation; but in chapter 19, filled with fear, he becomes the deserter of his nation. At one moment he can confront over 400 prophets of Baal, but at another he flees from the empty threats of one woman. In 18:41-45, on the top of Mount Carmel, he prays to the Lord for the "sound of the rushing of rain"; in 19:4 in the wilderness he prays that God would take away his life. Commentators have written that in one chapter we see the prophet at his best; in the other we see the prophet at his worst.[13]

In these accounts of the Scripture we can see evidence that the Bible really is God's word, not a production of men. Had it been a human

---

13 See for these contrasts Arthur W. Pink, *Elijah*, (Edinburgh: The Banner of Truth Trust, 2002), 190.

production, it would have continually magnified its heroes and drew a veil over their sins and failures. Here however they are honestly recorded. The fact is that Elijah as James 5:17 tell us "was a man with a nature like ours," so he himself was subject as we also are to the pressures and problems of life, to situations which can cause fear, to the possibility of failure and depression. Dark shadows had continued to close in around him.

The story of his distress must begin in ch. 18, following his triumph over "the 450 prophets of Baal and the 400 prophets of Asherah, who eat at Jezebel's table," (v.19). On Mount Carmel the false prophets were helpless as they sought to call down fire on their sacrifice from morning until evening. But at the time of the evening sacrifice as Elijah prayed for the offering, though it was saturated three times with water, which also ran down from the altar to fill the trench that had been dug around it, "the fire of the LORD fell and consumed the burnt offering and the wood and the stones and the dust, and licked up the water that was in the trench," (v.38). The prophets were slain, the three and one half year drought was over and the rains came. Then we are told:

THE HAND OF THE LORD WAS UPON HIM. 18:45-46

The hand of the Lord denotes his power, his enabling and blessing. In Ezra 8, in the account of those who returned with Ezra to Jerusalem we are told in v.31 that as they departed from the river Ahava God's hand "was on us, and he delivered us from the hand of the enemy and from ambushes all the way." In Acts 11:21 at Antioch when some of those scattered from Jerusalem because of persecution preached "the hand of the Lord was with them, and a great number who believed turned to the Lord." Here God's hand imparts strength, here swiftness in running so that Elijah can cover the 18 miles before the chariot bringing king Ahab can arrive. We also need God's hand upon us to strengthen us, to protect us; and we need his hand with us in our witness. He alone can move people to believe and turn to the Lord.

THE KING AND QUEEN WERE AGAINST HIM. 19:1-2

Ahab told Jezebel "all that Elijah had done, and how he had killed all the prophets with the sword," (v.1). There is a remarkable omission here for God is not mentioned; she was not told what God had done following the helplessness of all the false prophets, including her own. Nothing of the dousing of the evening sacrifice three times, the prayer of Elijah and then the fire licking up the water even in the trench dug around the altar. The tragedy is that God is not spoken of in the everyday lives of those who are unsaved – except as a swear word or occasionally when they are in trouble. We must endeavour to speak of him to them; to let them see how important he is in our daily lives. Jesus encouraged Legion, delivered from the possession of evil spirits, "Go home to your friends and tell them how much the Lord has done for you, and how he has had mercy upon you," (Mark 5:19).

As Pink[14] explains, neither judgments (the prophets slain) nor blessings (the abundant rain) will change the rebellious heart unless God's sovereign grace works in them. We need to cry to God for this. Here it is clear that Jezebel is full of rage at what has happened and unrepentant in spite of God's works. She was like a bear robbed of her cubs. She vows that she will have Elijah sought out and killed before the day is out! The same word from God can convict but also harden the heart – we think of the response of those who heard Isaiah preach when their hearts became "dull" and their ears "heavy," (Isa. 6:10) and also those who listened to Paul who quoted again this passage in Acts 28:23-28 testifying about the "kingdom of God" and about Jesus. Remember the warning given to the Hebrews, "Today, if you hear his voice, do not harden your hearts," (Heb. 4:7).

THE SITUATION GOT ON TOP OF HIM. 19:3

Jezebel threatened "by this time tomorrow." Elijah seems unable to view the threat calmly. Why give him a day and also warn him of her

---

[14] Pink, *Elijah*, 194.

intentions? It is likely this is only a threat. Would she dare to kill him? One remembers his popularity at that time – see 18:39, when God sent the fire, "And when all the people saw it, they fell on their faces and said, 'The LORD, he is God; the LORD, he is God.'" Is it possible that Jezebel wanted to drive him out, remove his influence? Yet we note Elijah's response, "Then he was afraid, and he arose and ran for his life."

Some commentators here suggest that no criticism should be attached to Elijah in quitting Jezreel. They point to how the Lord taught his disciples "When they persecute you in one town, flee to the next," (Matt. 10:23). They were not to expose themselves unnecessarily to danger. We recall how on occasions Paul and his companions in mission would move on when opposition was about to break out in real persecution e.g., Acts 14:5-6; 17:10, 14. Yet the way the flight is expressed "he was afraid and ran for his life" does not seem to convey just a counsel of prudence here. This was a crucial moment in the history of Israel what with the peoples' response on Carmel. They might have come out and possibly a genuine reformation could have begun. There was an opportunity missed which never came again. Leaving in "fear" is not leaving in wisdom to fight another day. There were a number of factors which suggest failure here with Elijah at this crucial moment.

Hurried action
In the past, we read "The word of the LORD came." In 17:2 following the word of the LORD, he tarried at the brook Cherith; also in v.8 he goes to Zarephath at "the word of the LORD"; again, in 18:1, "After many days the word of the LORD came to Elijah, in the third year, saying, 'Go, show yourself to Ahab, and I will send rain upon the earth.'" So time after time, he was told what to do. But now there was no waiting on such a word; he takes things into his own hands. We have noted that it was "the hand of the LORD" (1 Kings 18:46) that brought him to Jezreel and the Lord did not instruct him to leave.

Blessing may have resulted if he had stayed where God had brought him; but he acts quickly, not giving himself time to really think, and so without the guidance of God, decides to run. We need to wait upon God throughout all the path of life. Wait for him to guide, when to stay and when to move, in fact in all our decisions we need to pray for the guidance of God. Our actions will affect the whole of our lives. You should be careful lest you do this - take things into your own hands.

Overcome by fear

We read "He was afraid." Elijah is panic stricken and in fear he runs from only a threat. He ran for his life – not for God or the good of his people, when a work of reformation could have changed everything and the thousands that gathered on Mount Carmel would have taken a stand, but fled "for his life." He had lost his faith in God to protect him.

Faith in God and the fear of God are the only means of deliverance from crippling fear. In Isa. 8:13 we read, "But the LORD of hosts, him you shall honor as holy. Let him be your fear, and let him be your dread." Then you will have no-one to fear. Of Moses it is written, "By faith he left Egypt, not being afraid of the anger of the king, for he endured as seeing him who is invisible," (Heb. 11:27). If we trust in him we "will not be afraid," Isa. 12:2. So if we have the fear of the Lord in our hearts then we can be delivered from the fear of man. To the young Jeremiah at the time of his call, the Lord assured him, "Do not be afraid of them, for I am with you to deliver you, declares the LORD," Jer. 1:8.

It has often been pointed out that in the Scriptures often men have failed in the area of what is supposedly their greatest strength. Abraham the man of faith forsook the land to go down to Egypt and called Sarai his sister – they were related – but did not confess she was his wife, Gen. 12:10-20; Moses, the meekest man in all the earth (Num. 12:3) was angry, struck the rock and spoke rashly with his lips (Psa. 106:32-

33), saying things he should not have said; John the apostle of love, asked Jesus to call down fire on a Samaritan village, Luke 9:54; Peter faced the mob, drew his sword, but denied the Lord before a little maid, John 18:10-17. Now here Elijah who had boldly gone in before Ahab to announce the coming of the drought, 1 Kings 17:1 and faced 400 false prophets and 450 who sat at Jezebel's table, now flees from one woman and from purely one threat. They failed, all in the area of their greatest strength. Edinburgh Castle was captured from the English in 1314 by Thomas Randolph, first earl of Moray and a small band of twenty men. Because of the steepness of the rock it was thought to be impregnable from that side. Therefore no sentry was stationed there. One misty morning the small party climbed the steep hill, surprised the garrison and took the Castle from its strongest side. We need to be always on our guard and look to him. You cannot stand alone.

We should learn from Elijah that we have no strength apart from the Lord. If left to ourselves we are weak. He was a man of God, but the best of men are only men at the best. We may have many gifts and talents; we may be considered to be giants spiritually; we may have been greatly used, but let God's enabling power be withdrawn for a moment and we will be as weak as water. It was John Gill[15] who in 1697 wrote "Elijah's conduct on this occasion shows that the spirit and courage he had previously manifested were of the Lord, and not himself—and that those who have the greatest zeal and courage for God and His truth, if left to themselves, become weak and timorous." 2 Cor.4:7 reminds us "But we have this treasure in jars of clay, to show that the surpassing power belongs to God and not to us." The psalmist prays "Hold me up, that I may be safe..." Psa. 119:117. We remember also Peter in Matt. 14:30-31 when the boat was in the storm, he walked upon the water to go to Jesus, "but when he saw the wind, he was afraid, and

---

[15] www.biblestudytools.com/commentaries/gills-exposition-of-the-bible. Accessed July 2017.

beginning to sink he cried out, 'Lord save me.'" Jesus' hand was immediately stretched out to do just that. He said to Peter, "O you of little faith, why did you doubt?"

His physical state may have left him vulnerable

We do not often think about this but there is no doubt that the physical can affect the spiritual. Physical weakness, exhaustion, sickness can impact us spiritually. I recall occasions when I had opportunity to minister to believers who were seriously ill. Sometimes in their weakness they would need to be reassured of their acceptance with God. The devil has no compassion and in these dark hours would endeavour to make them doubt their salvation. It was so important in reading the Scriptures and ministering to them to major on the basic truths of salvation through the cross of Christ and the precious blood. Thank God for the sure promises of his word which they could hear again and continue to rest upon. The Lord's promise to me when I came to him as a child is still as certain now as it was then, when my mother first read it to me, "All that the Father gives me will come to me, and whoever comes to me I will never cast out," (John 6:37).

But what we are seeing here with Elijah is something deeper. What had occurred in chapter 18 – the challenge to Ahab, the confrontation with the false priests on Carmel, his prolonged intercession before the Lord for the rain, his supernatural running to Jezreel (about 17 miles) arriving before the king, who had travelled in a chariot - all was so physically demanding. The response of the King and Queen, the anger, rejection and threats meant his expectations for reformation and revival were dashed. So how do we see the prophet in chapter 19? He is fearful at the threat of Jezebel, disappointed, discouraged that repentance and revival have not happened and expresses his feelings of failure, vulnerability and self-pity. He has a sense of worthlessness, wants to escape, to cut himself off from people (vv.3-5 show him in Beersheba, a distance of around 100 miles, where he leaves his servant and sets out into the wilderness a day's journey). He is exhausted and sits down under a broom tree and even wants to die. The shadows close in around him and in the darkness of the situation he prays, "It is enough; now, O LORD, take away my life, for I am no better than my fathers," (v4). Most modern commentators see here the classic signs of depression. We will see the Lord's loving response below to his exhausted, disillusioned servant. It is important to note that for ourselves to sink into such a state costs us in terms of our physical, emotional happiness, our social relationships, whether it be in the home, the church or in the community and our effectiveness for God and his kingdom.

Often a mountain top experience like Carmel can be followed by a low emotional state. Two important comments are needed here. First, be on your guard particularly after a time of great blessing and be ready for an attack of the enemy. Second, remember that your spiritual life should not just be a matter of seeking to go from one spiritual high to another, one retreat or special conference/holiday to another, valuable as they may be. You need to determine to get involved in the local church and endeavour to walk with God in your daily life. Isa. 40:31 reminds us that by the Lord's strength we not only can "mount up with wings like eagles...run and not be weary" but we can go on in the hardest place of all, the daily routine of life i.e., we can "walk and not faint." It is on the ground and in the local situation that your spiritual input and effectiveness must be seen.

He was self reliant

Later in 19:9-10 we find three times the use of "I" i.e., "I have been very jealous for the LORD...and I, even I only, am left..." Did he see himself as the only one standing, the only faithful one? Was there some pride here? Is there a clue in v.4? "I am no better than my fathers". Has he been thinking that he was? He could do it, he could stand when they could not? Had not Elijah become self-reliant? Now he was learning that without the Lord's power and strength he was nothing, he was weak. 1 Cor. 10:12 warns us "Therefore let anyone who thinks that he stands take heed lest he fall."

THE LORD STILL CARED FOR HIM. 19:3-18

Elijah flees to Beersheba, to the far south. We are told first that he, "came to Beersheba, which belongs to Judah," 19:3. Did he think this would be a safe place for him to hide? Was he not now outside the territory governed by Ahab and Jezebel? But there his safety was not even certain, for at that time the kingdom of Judah was ruled by Jehoshaphat, and his son had married "the daughter of Ahab" (2 Kings 8:18). One should also note the close relationship between the house of Jehoshaphat and that of Ahab. When the former was asked to join the latter in an expedition against Ramoth-Gilead, Jehoshaphat, declared, "I am as you are, my people as your people, my horses as your horses," (22:4). If Jehoshaphat was contacted by Ahab and Jezebel he surely would be ready to hand over Elijah. So, even to have come to Beersheba would not save Elijah; he must flee yet farther. As we pointed out, he leaves his servant in Beersheba "But he himself went a day's journey into the wilderness and came and sat down under a broom tree. And he asked that he might die…" (19:4).

At Jezreel "he ran for his life" but now in the wilderness he prays "take away my life". As we noted, he is afraid, disappointed and discouraged at the lack of the lasting success of Carmel, overcome by feelings of failure; he is now exhausted with all his exertions, vulnerable, full of self-pity, with a sense of his own worthlessness. As the shadows have closed in around him he has attempted to escape, to cut himself off from people. Disillusioned, disappointed, he cries out "It is enough." He had forsaken the place into which God had brought him, the path of duty, taken things into his own hands. Elijah can fight no longer. "I am no better than my fathers." Either he was pleading his weakness, that there was a lack of fruit resulting from his ministry, or his failure, that he was no more successful than his fathers. Pink[16] finds here the results of giving way to fear and unbelief:

> See here once more the consequences which follow upon giving way to fear and unbelief. Poor Elijah was now in the slough of despond, an experience which few if any of the Lord's people escape at sometime or other. He had forsaken the place into which the Lord had brought him, and now was tasting the bitter effects of a course of self-will. All pleasure had gone out of life: the joy of the Lord was no longer his strength. What a rod we make for our backs when we deliberately depart from the path of duty. By leaving the paths of righteousness we cut ourselves off from the springs of spiritual refreshment and therefore the "wilderness" is now our dwelling place.

It is a good thing that sometimes God says no to our requests. Elijah asks, "take away my life" when God had planned to take him to heaven without dying. Here how precious it is to learn from vv.5-8 that the Lord had not deserted him in his time of need. The Lord had in no sense turned from his servant and abandoned him to suffer further from the effects of his own decisions and actions. Psa.103:10-13 reminds us that "He does not deal with us according to our sins, nor repay us according to our iniquities," (v. 10). Again v.13 assures us that "As a father shows compassion to his children, so the LORD shows compassion to those who fear him. For he knows our frame; he remembers that we are dust." The great shepherd cares for his sheep, even when they wander from him. Elijah lay down and slept and God allows him to sleep.

There are times when God can withhold sleep in his great purpose. In Psalm 77:4 we are told "You (God) hold my eyelids open" and we remember the case of Ahasuerus in Esther 6:1 "On that night the king could not sleep…" In Elijah's sleeping under the broom tree, we can see the gracious hand of God allowing his servant to begin to renew his strength. It was not God's design that his servant should die of exhaustion in the wilderness after his long, long flight from Jezreel.

---

[16] Pink, *Elijah*, 213.

There are times when "he gives to his beloved sleep" (Psalm 127:2). He sleeps until that moment the angel touched him saying "Arise and eat," (19:5). Here we have the 3rd provision for the prophet, not by ravens or a poor widow but by an angel! God still loved him. He sent an angel from his own great work to his servant "and behold, there was at his head a cake baked on hot stones and a jar of water," (19:6). We remember the ministry of angels to other servants of God; the angels that delivered Lot from Sodom before the city was destroyed by fire and brimstone (Gen. 19:15-16); the angel that "shut the lions' mouths" when Daniel was thrown into their den (Dan. 6:22); it was angels who carried Lazarus to "Abraham's side" (Luke 16:22); it was an angel which came to Peter in the prison, caused the chains to fall from his hands, and the iron gate of the city to "open for them of its own accord," (Acts 12:7-10); and it was an angel who assured Paul that in the storm "God has granted you all that sail with you," (Acts 27:23-24). Heb. 1:14 would lead us to consider that the ministry of angels "sent out to serve for the sake of those who are to inherit salvation" is not just something of the past, even if they do not appear as in OT times.

Elijah eats and the Lord allows him to lie down again. The Lord is refreshing the weary prophet. He is aware when our strength is gone and our energies are spent. This is a truly remarkable manifestation of the Lord's care of his wayward and exhausted servant. We noted already that in the past in chapter 17, the meat provided and the water he drank at the brook Cherith was not given by angels. The bread was brought by ravens! In Zarephath it was a widow who baked the cakes from the barrel of meal that did not fail. But here God assured Elijah of the constancy of his love and care in a very special way in that an angel ministered to him. You may ask why God showed such tender care to his servant. It was not because he condoned his sin, but because such an amazing demonstration of love was needed to assure the prophet God still cared for him. He would continue to comfort his heart and lead him to repentance.

It appears that when morning came the angel touched him again. Another provision was there for the prophet and "he ate and drank." All this again was special proof of God's tender love. He wanted him to know that he could lift him up again through repentance, to experience forgiveness and restore him to service. If you have failed God, here is a revelation of the love of your God. Realise that you can repent of your sins and cast yourself upon his love. 1 John 1:9 is his promise "If we confess our sins, he is faithful and just to forgive us our sins and to cleanse us from all unrighteousness." As far as Elijah was concerned, this caring ministry from the angel was so important, because ahead there was another journey.

THE JOURNEY WOULD BE TOO GREAT FOR HIM. 19:7

"Arise and eat, for the journey is too great for you." That is, too great for Elijah - without the Lord's help. The Lord was not finished with him. It is not God's will that his children give up, be discouraged, and leave their ministry or place of service. His servants do not retire before their work is done. We are to finish the work God has given us to do. But it appears that Elijah has not yet reached the point of submission and renewed obedience. Yet God was still providing and caring for his wayward servant. That morning the angel had come to him "a second time and touched him." How great is the Lord's patience and how enduring his love and grace. When away in heart from God we can be slow to recognise and respond to his love and persist in our disobedience and sin. We recall in Psa. 32:3-5 how when David "kept silent" his "bones wasted away." God's hand was "heavy upon him" and his "strength was dried up as by the heat of summer" until he confessed his transgressions to the LORD. Elijah, in his backslidden state seems to have accepted God's gracious provision and remains unresponsive as far as any expression of remorse, gratitude or thanksgiving was concerned. Pink[17] can remind us that:

---

[17] Pink, *Elijah*, 226.

When the heart is estranged from God, when self becomes the center and circumference of our interests, a hardness and deadness steals over us so that we are impervious unto the Lord's goodness. Our vision is dimmed so that we no longer perceive whose gracious Hand it is which is ministering to us. Our affections are chilled so that we no longer appreciate the benefits bestowed upon us. We become indifferent, callous, unresponsive. We descend to the level of the beasts, consuming what is given us with no thought of the Creator's faithfulness.

First, Elijah could eat and drink and lie down again; now he "ate and drank, and went in the strength of that food forty days and nights to Horeb, the mount of God," (19:8) – again not recognising the miraculous provision God had made to strengthen him. There was a cave there in Horeb into which he entered to hide. He is still fleeing from Jezebel. But God has not abandoned him in his darkness and depth of despair.

GOD IN GRACE RECOMISSIONED HIM. 19:9-21

It was at that moment we read "And behold, the word of the LORD came to him" (19:9). God had spoken to him like this before. We noted how the word of the Lord had directed him to hide by the brook Cherith, (17:2-3); it had come to him again bidding him to journey to Zarephath to be fed by the widow, (17:8-9); it also had commanded him to show himself unto Ahab, (18:1). Now as he hides away in the cave that same communication comes to him again. The Lord says to him, "What are you doing here, Elijah?" (19:9). Note the earlier occasions when God spoke to him. Concerning Elijah's time at the brook Cherith he said "I have commanded the ravens to feed you there" (18:4); also the direction to Zarephath, to the destitute widow, "I have commanded a widow there to feed you" (18:9). But now God asks him "What are you doing here?" He had run away, turning aside from the path of duty and where God had wanted him to be, away from the land of Israel, from his people and the work of renewal. God knows where His servants are, what they are doing and not doing. He is the omniscient God and "The eyes of the LORD are in every place," (Prov. 15:3). This question must have come as a challenge and even a rebuke for his conscience.

"What are you doing here?" Are we "doing" anything for God or are we totally inactive or are we really doing what he has purposed for us to do? Are we "here" when we should be "there"? As far as Elijah was concerned, he was the Lord's servant; and had been mightily used as God's power had been in evidence in his ministry. God challenges him "What are you doing here?" Could God not have protected him in Jezreel?

"He said, I have been very jealous for the LORD, the God of hosts. For the people of Israel have forsaken your covenant, thrown down your altars, and killed your prophets with the sword, and I, even I only, am left, and they seek my life, to take it away," (19:10). The confession "I have been very jealous for the LORD, the God of hosts" was true, for with his great desire for the glory of God, he had not shrunk back from the most challenging service and witness for his Master. He had been deeply distressed at how the people and their leaders had transgressed the law, forsaken the covenant, despised the worship of God for lifeless idols and brutally slew his prophets. But he had come to be convinced that it was all to no avail. "I, even I only, am left." In his opinion it was hopeless; he had laboured in vain and spent his strength for nothing and the message from Jezebel confirmed this. "They seek my life, to take it away." Here was a heart-rending confession of failure. This is what made him flee, disillusioned, discouraged, full of self-pity, convinced that his whole ministry had been in vain. Deep and dark shadows had enveloped him. But God had not given up on him.

"And he said, 'Go out and stand on the mount before the LORD.' And, behold, the LORD passed by..." (19:11). Horeb, "the mount of God" (v.8) (often referred to as Sinai) was a special place in the history of the nation in earlier times in the OT. It was there that the Lord appeared to Moses at the burning bush, (Exod. 3:1-4) and where the law was given to Israel, (Deut. 4:15). One recalls the record of Exod. 19:16 "there were thunders and lightnings and a thick cloud on the mountain"; Deut. 4:11 "the mountain burned with fire to the heart of heaven, wrapped in darkness, cloud, and gloom." It was a place where the presence of God was particularly manifested with all the above phenomena. Heb. 12:18 refers to "a blazing fire and darkness and gloom and a tempest." As Elijah stood on the mountain we learn, "And behold, the LORD passed by, and a great and strong wind tore the mountains and broke in pieces the rocks before the LORD, but the LORD was not in the wind. And after the wind an earthquake, but the LORD was not in the earthquake. And after the earthquake a fire, but the LORD was not in the fire. And after the fire the sound of a low whisper," (19:11-12). Here was a powerful display of God's power, terrible, frightening and awe-inspiring. But what was this meant to convey to Elijah? We can connect these striking manifestations of God's power with the situation and future ministry of the prophet himself.

This frightening display of God's power should be linked to the directions given to Elijah in 19:15-18. The message which followed actually was the interpretation of the former manifestations. It can be maintained that God was in grace revealing the future to Elijah, a future which is quite remarkable. We remember the words of Amos 3:7 "For the Lord LORD does nothing without revealing his secret to his servants the prophets." This is exactly what occurred there on Horeb. Through these powerful manifestations God was graciously revealing what was to come to Elijah. In a verse or two we find the Lord directing Elijah to anoint Hazael over Syria, Jehu over Israel, and Elisha to be prophet in his place, assuring him that, "the one who escapes from the sword of Hazael shall Jehu put to death, and the one who escapes from the sword of Jehu shall Elisha put to death," (19:17).

This was the prophetic meaning of the solemn manifestations Elijah had witnessed - they were pointing to the judgments God would bring upon the apostate nation. Thus the strong "wind" was a figure of the terrible retribution which Hazael brought upon Israel, (2Kings 8:12); the "earthquake" was a picture of the revolution under Jehu, when he struck down the house of Ahab, (2 Kings 9:7-10) and the "fire" depicted the work of judgment completed by Elisha. But it is important to note that all of this was designed to assure Elijah his disheartened servant that God was still sovereign and in control. The judgments were to fall upon guilty Israel, yet as we will see shortly, there would still be a remnant – seven thousand men - for in wrath the Lord would remember mercy. The chosen nation would not be completely wiped out, (19:18). Sadly, that was still to come. In 2 Kings 13:23 we read that after Hazael had oppressed Israel all the days of Jehoahaz, "But the LORD was gracious to them and had compassion on them, and he turned towards them, because of his covenant with Abraham, Isaac, and Jacob, and would not destroy them, nor has he cast them from his presence until now." This was finally to happen to Israel in 2 Kings 17. So the "strong wind," the "earthquake" and the "fire" were symbolic portents of the judgments which God was shortly to send upon his idolatrous people. But there was in the revelation also the "low whisper" which was intended particularly for the prophet.

Elijah goes out again. Having heard the low whisper, we are told "he wrapped his face in the cloak and went out and stood at the entrance to the cave," (v.13). God is seeking still in grace to reach and recover his servant Elijah. The Lord speaks to his servant quietly – not in anger - reassuring him that he is in control and to encourage his despondent spirit. He has not forsaken him. The wrapping of his face in his mantle indicates Elijah's response. We see his reverence for the almighty and his sense of his own unworthiness—as the seraphim were said to cover their faces in the Lord's presence (Isa. 6:2, 3); as Abraham when he found himself in the presence of God said, "Behold, I have undertaken to speak to the Lord, I who am but dust and ashes," (Gen. 18:27); or as Moses when at the burning bush he "hid his face, for he was afraid to look at God," (Exod. 3:6).

Once again the Lord speaks to him, "What are you doing here, Elijah?" The Lord is reminding him again of the importance of being where God would direct him to be, where to serve and where to witness. God is very graciously dealing with him still. He will need to be available to go where God wants him to go. Elijah repeats again his passionate commitment in the past, his isolation and frustration as he sought to see the nation return to worship and to glorify the Lord, (19:13-14). God in his grace has not set him aside but recalls him to serve and to act on his behalf. He is recommissioned and asked to journey from the extreme south (Horeb) to the extreme north (Damascus) (with Jezebel still out to kill him) to anoint Hazael king over Syria and Jehu over Israel and also to commission Elisha to be the prophet who was to carry on the witness of God. Finally, in v.18 he gives to Elijah what was in effect a promise, "Yet I will leave seven thousand in Israel, all the knees that have not bowed unto Baal, and every mouth that has not kissed him," (19:18).

There are differences of opinion of the significance of this verse. The KJV has "I have left me…" Most will probably find here a rebuke to Elijah – his statement "I, even I only, am left…" suggesting that God corrects him, telling him that there are thousands who follow the Lord! But there is an alternative reading of this statement in the margin of the KJV "I will leave…" and this is the translation of the ESV[18] and can be how we understand the Hebrew. So there are two possibilities. Either God is reassuring Elijah that his work was more successful than he ever realized and was not in vain; or he is giving him a promise of the blessing that would follow future ministry, his and that by Elisha. Rather than suggest that this refers to past blessing – surely Elijah would know of seven thousand others? – it is an encouragement, a

---

[18] Also the LXX renders "and thou shalt leave in Israel…"

promise for what is yet to come. Pink[19] also interprets these verses in this sense:

> Rather do we regard these verses as a record of God's comforting answer to the Prophet's despondency. Elijah felt that the forces of evil had triumphed: the Lord announces that the worship of Baal should be utterly destroyed (1Ki 19:17 and cf. 2Ki 10:25-28). Elijah grieved because he "only was left": the Lord declares, "I will leave me seven thousand in Israel." So desperate was the situation, they sought to take the life of Elijah: the Lord promises that Elisha shall complete his mission. Thus did Jehovah most tenderly silence Elijah's fears and reassure his heart. In view of the promise in 1 Kings 19:18, we may conclude the blessing of the Lord rested upon their labours and that not a few were converted.

Elijah responded to the call and promise of God. The dark despondency of the past was at an end and he submitted again to the Lord's direction. "So he departed from there." (19:19). There are two strands of evidence to the fact that Elijah was not now being set aside and replaced, however you read v.16. When Elijah "cast his cloak" over Elisha, we are informed that "he arose and went after Elijah and assisted (not replaced) him," (19:21). Also in 21:17-18 God sends Elijah again to Ahab, i.e., he recommissions him. "Then the word of the LORD came to Elijah the Tishbite, saying, 'Arise, go down to meet Ahab...And you shall say unto him, 'Thus says the LORD'...'" God has not cast him aside; he has been reinstated and used. He now also has a young man as his companion who will initially help him with the winning of the seven thousand, until the time comes for him to ascend into heaven on the chariot of fire, (2 Kings 2:11).

We see that it is not God's will for his children to be disheartened, to wallow in darkness or the deep shadows of hopelessness and defeat and finally, to give up. It is not in line with his word for his servants to retire until their work is done. If God has entrusted us with a work to

---

[19] Pink, *Elijah*, 249-250.

finish we must not abandon it - even if we are afraid or feel that we have failed. In the darkness of our situation or circumstance God gently whispers to us to leave our hiding place and start again. There is always hope.

Elijah had run away from God's work in fear, but in the darkness of his despair God cared for him and offered him bread and water. When he moved to the cave at Horeb he graciously revealed to him his future purpose. God's whisper came to him again. However, God didn't say, "You can just stay here as long as you want." Instead, God told his prophet, "Go return," (19:15). We read of Elijah "So he departed" (19:19). God tells us, his children, to go back to the work. Back to the painful situation, to those difficult people. Back to the service each of us has been equipped to complete. The gentle whisper reminded Elijah that, as far as God was concerned, the place of discouragement could become the place of beginning again. The dark shadows can be dispelled with God's shining light to direct our way.

Remember Abraham when his faith was tested and he forsook the land of Canaan for Egypt in Gen. 12:10? The time came when we read, "And he journeyed on from the Negeb as far as Bethel to the place where his tent had been at the beginning, between Bethel and Ai, to the place where he had made an altar at the first. And there Abram called upon the name of the LORD," (Gen. 13:3-4). Elijah must go back the way he came to the land of Israel, all the way to Damascus. We noted earlier that when Peter had so sadly denied his Lord, the Lord met with him in secret first and then at the sea of Tiberius he recommissioned him "Tend my sheep," (John 21:16). Here similarly, Elijah must be the instrument for the fulfilment of God's promise concerning the seven thousand. There is hope for you to begin again, to be an instrument again, to be used again. With Jesus we will always have enough to start again.

CHAPTER TWELVE

Hope for the Unknown Future

Psa. 147:5; Mark 14:62

WE DO NOT know what the future days will hold for us. There could be difficult times, dark shadows falling across our path; all is unknown. But we have hope, because we have him. We have an omniscient and omnipotent God, i.e., a God who knows all things and is all powerful. Concerning the fact that he is omniscient, this is affirmed in many scriptures as we will see. Again, scholars divide the word omnipotence in this way; first, omni which means "all" and potens meaning "powerful." So we also have an all-powerful God. Let us consider both of these amazing attributes of God – first omniscience. Note:

IN THE SCRIPTURES GOD'S OMNISCIENCE IS DECLARED

Many scriptures affirm this. For example, Psa. 147:5 "Great is the Lord, and abundant in power, his understanding is beyond measure." Again, Isa. 40:26 of the starry host, he knows them "by number, calling them all by name." Man knows little yet about the universe but God knows the number and the individual characteristics of every star in the entire universe! Therefore he knows everything about you. Isa. 46:9-10 assures us that God knows what will occur until the very end of history itself, "I am God, and there is no other; I am God and there is none like me, declaring the end from the beginning and from ancient times things not yet done." Remember Psa. 139:1-4, where we discover that he also knows everything about us; our actions; our thoughts; our path; our resting place; our words, even our life from its very beginning in the womb. Daniel also reminds us that "He knows what is in the darkness," (Dan. 2:22). Nothing is hidden from him. Though he is invisible to us, we are not in any sense to him. Concerning Israel, God says, "I remember all their evil," Hosea 7:2; also, in Ezek. 11:5 God says, "For I know the things that come into your mind." Heb. 4:13 reminds us that "no creature is hidden from his sight, but all are naked and exposed to the eyes of him to whom we must give account." Finally, Prov. 15:3 states, "The eyes of the Lord are in every place, keeping watch on the evil and the good."

We draw upon A. W. Pink[20] The Attributes of God, not to quote but to summarise. He knows everything which happens in every part of his vast domain. He also is perfectly aware of everything to come, every event from the least to the greatest in the future. The divine knowledge of the future is linked to his purpose. And the accomplishment of what he has purposed is guaranteed (his omnipotence). What he has purposed he will do. Prov. 19:21, affirms "Many are the plans in the mind of a man, but it is the purpose of the Lord that will stand." So his knowledge is linked to the fact that he has ordained it, willed it and will bring it to pass.

BY SOME SCHOLARS HIS OMNISCIENCE IS DOUBTED

The modern debate about God's complete knowledge has been around for approximately thirty years or so. It has been entitled "Open Theism". The issue can involve a whole range of subjects, but we will try to focus upon the discussion as it relates to our theme.

In terms of God's knowledge the argument is that, if God were able to know everything in advance, all would be fixed and there would be no place for human freedom and decision-making. In effect, would we not be trapped in a fully-determined universe, dominated by an absolute fatalism?

---

[20] A. W. Pink, *The Attributes of God*, (Grand Rapids, MI, Baker Books, 1975), 21-26.

In The Openness of God by Clark Pinnock et al,[21] we read, "God knows what he needs to know to deal with any contingency that might arise, but does not know or need to know every detail of the future." This view implies that God learns things and then insists that God enjoys learning them – indeed, "he is the best learner of all, because he is completely open to all the input of an unfolding world."

Open Theists often focus on what they see as the apparent injustice of the idea of God allowing great evils to happen – the holocaust of the 1930s and 1940s under Hitler, the genocide in Rwanda in the early 1990s or the awful famine in Ethiopia in 1983-4. We could add events in the war in Syria and the migrants. A God, who knew in advance of these things and then allowed them to happen, does not come up to what is the standard of justice they expect of God. The open view of God seems to ease the problem by enabling them to say that he didn't know these things would happen and so cannot be blamed for them! As someone has said, it's an attempt "to let God off the hook."

We must remember that God is a moral being, who interacts with all he has himself created – men, angels and even demons. He has given men a great deal of freedom and then he pleads with and persuades them; he threatens them and punishes their sins; he rewards and blesses them. He cannot be blamed for man's actions. Why the world is as it is with its evil, suffering and pain is made clear by a passage as found in Rom. 1:18-32 and in the statements "God gave them up," (vv. 24, 26, 28).

THERE WAS A REVELATION OF GOD to the Gentile Nations. v.19
"For what can be known about God is plain to them…"
God provided man with ample evidence of his existence. God also equipped man with the faculties and powers to comprehend or receive

---

[21]   Clark Pinnock, *The Openness of God: A Biblical Challenge to the Traditional Understanding of God*, by Clark Pinnock, Richard Rice, John Sanders, William Hasker, and David Basinger (Downers Grove, IL: InterVarsity Press, 1994), 123-124.

the evidence of his existence and what could be known of him. Where? In creation, v.20, "his eternal power and divine nature, have been clearly perceived, ever since the creation of the world, in the things that have been made." So the God of creation was known before the flood.

THERE WAS A CLEAR REJECTION OF GOD by the Gentile Nations. v.21

"For although they knew God, they did not honour him as God or give thanks to him." They had a knowledge of his existence, but when they should have given their whole being over to him they did not. Instead they refused him the gratitude and worship to which he was due. So we have a picture of the multitude of the nations refusing to recognise him – receiving from his hand daily while not returning even one thanksgiving. They became conceited and vain in their reasoning, with their questions and speculations. We see clearly the outcome:

(a) Ignorance vv.21-22 "their foolish hearts were darkened." Their speculations instead of leading them nearer to God were the means of darkening their minds and blinding them even more. The knowledge of God was lost by succeeding generations.

(b) Idolatry v.23 The fact was that men could not stand the knowledge of God for it made them uncomfortable in their sin. So they turned away to host lesser deities with their ideas of God embodied in images of men, even birds, beasts and the lowest reptiles.

THERE WAS A RESULT FROM GOD vv.24-31

"God gave them up."

We need to note the statement with which this section began. In v.18 Paul tells us that "the wrath of God is revealed" and the present tense is used. No doubt that there is future wrath as in 2:16 where Paul writes of "that day when, according to my gospel, God judges the secrets of men by Christ Jesus." But here it is the present wrath being revealed as God gave men and women up to follow their own rebellious way, handing sinners over to themselves. They gave up God; so he gave them up. He leaves them to themselves, resulting in moral and spiritual degeneration, which is to be seen as a judicial act of God. He gives them over to (a) sexual impurity (v.24), where their lust was given free rein to dishonour their bodies; (b) shameful lusts (vv.25-27) which Paul sees expressed in lesbian practices (v.26) and homosexual relationships (v.27) and (c) a depraved mind (v.28) preferring to forget about God, which results in all kinds of anti-social behaviour, described in a list of 21 vices (vv.29-31). They do things which ought not to be done, things not befitting the universe of the blessed God. They are filled with all kinds of unrighteousness, evil (engaging in destructive, hostile activities), covetousness (they must have more and are making gain even at the expense of others), having an attitude of malice (a desire to injure). They are full of envy, murder, strife (beating others down in continuous wrangling and contention), deceit, maliciousness (taking all things in an evil sense). They are gossips (secret slanderers), (open) slanderers, haters of God (manifesting as well as feeling such hatred), insolent (people who take pleasure in insulting others), haughty, boastful, inventors of evil (Jer. 19:5 speaks of things hardly imaginable), disobedient to parents (they will not be persuaded or listen to reason), foolish (showing no proper moral discernment), faithless (or covenant breakers, with no intention of carrying out their promises), heartless, ruthless (they cannot be restrained or cease in their hostilities to one another; they are unmerciful). Also v.32, despite the witness of conscience, they continue and even applaud and enjoy the vileness of the actions or the words of others. Here we see the depth of their corruption. What a picture! What guilt! So they did not want God but wanted their own way; so he let them go their own way. It is clear that man himself is responsible for much of the pain and wickedness in the world.

Again, we need to remember that many of the predictions given through God's servants, the prophets, were conditional and were only fulfilled if the condition was met – "if my people who are called by my name humble themselves, ... then I will ..." (2 Chron. 7:14). Sometimes the condition is not recorded, but has to be assumed by the reader. Also, when Jonah preached in Nineveh, "Yet forty days, and Nineveh will be overthrown!" (Jonah 3:4), there was a condition although unstated i.e., "if there is no repentance." That condition must have been part of the message of God through Jonah, and we know that at this time the Ninevites repented and the judgment was not carried out. These conditional pronouncements meant that men had the opportunity to make choices; but it is clear that the choices they finally made were foreknown by God. So there is continual interaction between God and men on earth, but the Bible affirms again and again that he knows the end from the beginning. God is and must be eternally omniscient.

Open theists also have problems with the cross and the doctrine of the atonement. These were highlighted back in 2000 by Robert Brow,[22] a Canadian theologian, in Christianity Today. In his article he explains the view of open theists, 'the cross was not a judicial payment" but is merely a visible space-time expression of how Christ has always suffered for our sins. He suffers alongside the sinner, rather than in the sinner's stead. So how can it be a payment? The Son of God was eternally both Lion and Servant, Shepherd and Lamb. He did not become Lamb simply when he was put on the cross. For open theists his identity as Lamb was eternal in the sense that he was already absorbing our sin and its consequences from the time the first creatures were made in the image of God.

But 1 Pet. 1:19-20, while it reveals that the lamb, without blemish was "foreknown before the foundation of the world" it was not from eternity or throughout the whole time until he was "made manifest" that he suffered alongside the sinner. 1 Pet. 2:24 affirms "he himself bore our sins in his own body on the tree" – not to the tree. There are many references in Scripture that appear best interpreted as revealing

---

[22] Robert Brow, "Evangelical Megashift" *Christianity Today* Feb. 19, 1990, 12-14.

that Christ was a substitute for sinners on the cross. Also that Jesus was "delivered up" to the cross "according to the definite plan and foreknowledge of God" to be crucified for sinners as a substitutionary atonement (Acts 2:23).

SUCH A REVELATION SHOULD LEAD HIS PEOPLE TO DEVOTION

As a demonstration of his omniscience the Lord affirms that he even knows when the sparrow falls or when we lose a single hair, (Matt. 10:29-30). So what can we say about this truth of God's omniscience?

It brings comfort. Job in chapter 23 knew that God was there and everywhere present. He could not find him so that he could spread out his case before him. But he still can console himself with this conviction in v10, 'He knows the way that I take…' Oh the comfort that God knows all about you.

It brings encouragement and faith to pray. There is no danger of being overlooked. Isa. 40:27 insists that our way is not "hidden from the LORD."

It also brings assurance to us. God foresaw the fall of man, our rebellion and sin and in the council chambers of eternity planned salvation, 1 Peter 1:18-21 the lamb was "foreknown before the foundation of the world." God knows all that is to come; he knows the end from the beginning.

God's eyes are always upon us. In Gen. 16:6-14 with Hagar, the servant of Sarai, God saw her when she fled. "So she called the name of the LORD who spoke to her, 'You are a God of seeing,' for she said, 'Truly here I have seen him who looks after me,'" (16:13). Also in 21:15-19, we learn that God saw and heard the boy Ishmael cry as he lay "under one of the bushes." So if we find ourselves in deep shadows, they do not envelop us, hiding us from him!

Again, we must note that he is not only Omniscient but Omnipotent! See:

THE WONDER OF GOD'S OMNIPOTENCE

Remember Dan. 4:35 where Daniel affirms of him, "all the inhabitants of the earth are accounted as nothing, and he does according to his will among the host of heaven and among the inhabitants of the earth; and none can stay his hand or say to him 'What have you done?'" Power is actually God's name, for in Mark 14:62 Jesus speaks of "seated at the right hand of Power." Power and God are inseparable.

We must see his complete independence of all created things, Job 38:4-6 teaches us that he "laid the foundations of the earth" and "determined its measurements" sunk its bases and "laid its cornerstone." Also in Job 26:14 we are told that in it all we get but a glimpse of his power – "the outskirts of his ways" or only a small "whisper" of him. So only a little part of his ways is seen in all that he does. In attempting to describe God's power there is always so much more to conceive. Again in Hab. 3:4 when the prophet saw in a vision the mighty God scattering the hills and overturning the mountains, we might think that in this we have a mighty demonstration of his power. Instead we learn that "there he veiled his power," rather than gave a demonstration of it. As Pink[23] affirms, "so inconceivable, so immense, so uncontrollable is the power of deity that the fearful convulsions which he works in nature 'conceal' more than they reveal of his infinite might."

The psalmist can remind us in Psa. 62:11 "Power belongs unto God." We can add, and to him alone. Not a creature in the entire universe has an atom of power only what God himself delegates. Everything consistent with his character God can do. It is true that there are some things he cannot do. He "never lies," Tit. 1:2; In Psa. 89:35 the Lord swears by his holiness "I will not lie to David"; again he cannot change. In Mal. 3:6 he reminds us, "For I the LORD do not change"; and he cannot fail his people. In Isa. 43:13 he affirms, "I work, and who can turn it back?" But the point here is that his power is unlimited.

---

[23] Pink, *The Attributes of God*, 58.

THE BREADTH OF HIS OMNIPOTENCE

Look at his omnipotence in CREATION. He has complete power over creation. In Job 9:8-10 he is the one "who alone stretched out the heavens and trampled the waves of the sea; who made the Bear and Orion, the Pleiades and the chambers of the south." In Psa. 104:3, all are under his feet "he makes the clouds his chariot; he rides on the wings of the wind," i.e., everything is under his perfect control. Before man can work he must have tools and materials, but God can begin with nothing and by his word out of nothing made all things "For he spoke, and it came to be; he commanded, and it stood firm," (Psa. 33:9) and in Rom. 4:17, "he calls into existence the things that do not exist."

In PRESERVATION.

It is certain that no creature has power to preserve itself. It is God who has "kept our soul among the living," Psa. 66:9 and in fact, "upholds the universe by the word of his power," Heb. 1:3.

In JUDGMENT.

Ezek. 22:14 states "can your courage endure, or can your hands be strong, in the days that I shall deal with you? I the LORD have spoken, and I will do it." In Acts 17:31 Paul assures us that God has "fixed a day on which he will judge the world." His power in raising the Lord Jesus is the confirmation that he will call all men to stand before him.

In RESURRECTION.

As we have noted, he can raise the dead. Paul reminds his audience before King Agrippa "Why is it thought incredible by any of you that God raises the dead?" (Acts 26:8). The sea, Death and Hell will give up their dead to be judged "each one of them," Rev. 20:13.

In RECREATION.

Rom. 8:21 affirms that "the creation itself will be set free from its bondage to corruption and obtain the freedom of the glory of the children of God." God will sort out this fallen world. "We are waiting for new heavens and a new earth in which righteousness dwells," 2 Peter 3:13.

In SALVATION.
It is gloriously possible for lives to be changed by the power of God. By that power we can become "partakers of the divine nature," 2 Pet. 1:3-4.

In his POWER TO KEEP US.
Concerning every one of his people, "no-one is able to snatch them out of the Father's hand," John 10:28-29. We should adore such a wonderful God. And yet there is more.

THE BLESSING OF HIS OMNIPOTENCE
Luke 1:37 reminds us how the angel who visited Mary could reflect over what God had done in the blessing he gave to Elizabeth that "nothing will be impossible with God." Jesus also assures his disciples, "with God all things are possible," Matt. 19:26. So you can trust such a God. What blessing he can bring to us! We have a God who can:

EMPOWER OUR WALK
In Eph. 1:19-20 Paul reminds us of "the immeasurable greatness of his power" which is "towards us who believe." It is "according to the working of his great might that he worked in Christ when he raised him from the dead and seated him at his right hand in the heavenly places." So that omnipotent power is available for us!

ENCOURAGE OUR FAITH
Eph. 3:20 sets before us that the God we pray to "is able to do far more abundantly than all we ask or think, according to the power at work within us." He is able to do things, but do them "far more abundantly"

than not just "all we ask" but even the things we "think" but have not
dared to ask!

MEET OUR NEEDS

Again, Phil. 4:19 assures us that God will supply every need of yours,
not out of, but "according to his riches in glory in Christ Jesus."

RENEW OUR STRENGTH

As we noted earlier, Isa. 40:29-31 reveals to us God's promise that he
"gives power to the faint" and "strength" to those who have no might.
As his people look to their great God in faith, relying on him, he will
"renew their strength" enabling them to "mount up with wings like
eagles" and causing them to experience the ability to accomplish things
that are supernatural – running and not being weary; also he gives them
the power to live in the daily routine of life – "they shall walk and not
faint."

REMOVE OUR FEARS (CONCERNING THE FUTURE)

as far as his purpose is concerned we need not fear. We can face the
unknown future will a sense of certainty; we can shout "Hallelujah!"
because we know from Rev. 19:6 "the Lord our God the Almighty
reigns." The future is all in his hands. What he has planned for our
universe he will bring to pass. As we see also in Rev. 5:7, the Lamb
took the scroll, which means that he will fulfil for this whole universe
what he has won through the cross.

Finally he will:

UPHOLD US EVERY DAY

Deut. 33:27 calls upon us to remember that "underneath are the
everlasting arms." He never will fail you – every day, "as your days, so
shall your strength be," Deut. 33:25. Seek to "walk with God," as Enoch
did, Gen. 5:22. Let him dispel the shadows.

CHAPTER THIRTEEN

Hope Through the Precious Blood

Hebrews 12:24 Blood that Speaks a Better Word

HERE WE HAVE a wonderful text. The whole passage is focused on the coming of the people of God to Mount Zion, the city of God. Jesus is of course the way - through his sacrifice. The OT priests stood daily "offering repeatedly the same sacrifices, which can never take away sins." Christ's sacrifice accomplished what theirs could never accomplish, "when Christ had offered for all time a single sacrifice for sins, he sat down at the right hand of God," (Heb. 10:11-12). This single, all-sufficient sacrifice for sin is the basis upon which we receive the blessings of the New Covenant (Heb. 10:16), regeneration, with the law written upon the heart and a God who by a divine act forgets forever our "sins and lawless deeds." They are remembered "no more," (v.17). Here in chapter 12 Jesus is the "mediator of the new covenant" and of his precious blood we are told that it "speaks a better word than the blood of Abel," (v.24).

Such a contrast is set before us here! Gen. 4 gives us the account of Cain murdering Abel, the man of faith. God speaks to Cain and says to him, "What have you done? The voice of your brother's blood is crying to me from the ground," (4:10). That blood was crying out for justice, judgment upon Cain. Here we learn that the precious blood of Christ "speaks a better word." So what is that word? We must enumerate the blessings which have come through that precious blood. It is:

BLOOD THAT SPEAKS PEACE

In Col.1:20 Paul writes of the Lord Jesus and the blessing of reconciliation he can bring to "things whether on earth or in heaven." Before reconciliation there was hostility – remember Rom. 5:10 which states that until we were reconciled "we were enemies." As sinners, our hearts were really hostile to God. We pushed him away, determined to run our own lives and do just what we wanted to do, say what we wanted to say etc. We had put self on the throne of our lives, not God. Again and again we have pointed out in these chapters that for this rebellion we only deserved God's judgment. We have highlighted the wonder of what God has done - that when we could not get right with God by ourselves, he himself took the initiative and sent his son! Here we are learning what his death for us has made possible "making peace by the blood of his cross." He has so taken our indebtedness upon himself that by the shedding of his blood he has removed all obstacles to us entering into peace with God. We must believe the good news of what Christ has done by his death on the cross, repent or turn from our rebellion and, trusting in Christ alone and his saving work, submit our lives to him. Then we have this blessing of peace, not wrath. But his blood is also:

BLOOD THAT BRINGS REDEMPTION

Among all the blessings with which God blesses his people we are told, "In him we have redemption through his blood, the forgiveness of our trespasses, according to the riches of his grace," (Eph. 1:7). Redemption was a familiar concept in the ancient world and in Judaism. The Jews knew of the work of a "kinsman redeemer" and redemption of property and people. For example, Naomi could say to her daughter-in-law Ruth regarding Boaz, "the man is a close relative of ours, one of our redeemers," (Ruth 2:20). Note also Leviticus 25:47-49, where an Israelite who has had to sell himself into slavery because of poverty could be redeemed. Also property sold could likewise be redeemed, making it possible for it to be kept within the family (Lev. 25: 24-25; Ruth 4: 1-6; Jer. 32: 6-9). In the Greek and Roman world, a slave or prisoner could also be redeemed, by the paying of a price. For example, slaves (whether born in slavery or bought into it) were allowed to buy their freedom (or for that freedom to be bought for them) via the intermediary of a pagan god. The money would be deposited in the pagan temple and the idea was that the slave would be released from his master on behalf of the god of the temple. The slave was bought "for freedom" (the technical term that was used). Inscriptions within the temples themselves have survived which are records of such transactions. So Christ has redeemed us by the paying of a price, and what a price! Precious blood. In Eph. 1:7 we have the blessing of forgiveness, freedom from guilt. We did not deserve this; our deliverance is "according to the riches of his grace." It is a blessing which we have "in him," when he becomes our saviour. But there are more blessings.

BLOOD THAT JUSTIFIES

Paul in Rom. 5:9 reminds us that "we have now been justified by his blood…" Justification means being declared not guilty and then accepted as righteous because of the righteousness of Christ which is put to our account. The reference to "his blood," affirms that it is a blessing which is also ours because Christ died for us. In Rom. 4:2-5 we learn that Abraham would have something to boast about – if he had been accepted by his own works. But rather he "believed God" and God affirmed his righteousness by faith. So we also hear the word of the gospel of good news, that all that needs to be done for our acceptance Christ has completed it on the cross and we come to believe and trust alone for acceptance in him. In vv.4-5 Paul explains further, "now to the one who works, his wages are not counted as a gift but as his due. And to the one who does not work but believes in him who justifies the ungodly, his faith is counted as righteousness." Sometimes when we are caused to think about eternity – perhaps we have had a serious illness, or even a near accident, or someone known to us dies unexpectedly – we change and start to do more, be more regular in our church attendance, or we do good works, thinking it might help us at the end. But this verse says something quite startling. It we are ever to find acceptance it is not that we must START WORKING but STOP. The blessing is to "the one who does not work," but puts his faith in a work done for him, by Christ, on the cross. We need to "believe", yes believe in the God who actually justifies by faith in Christ – through precious blood. This is God's way of salvation and rules out us having anything to boast in – we are only "ungodly" (4:5) and are accepted by his grace, when we actually only deserve the opposite i.e., judgment.

BLOOD THAT REMOVES WRATH

It is quite clear that all we deserve from God is his wrath. This wrath is often referred to in the earlier chapters of Romans (1:18; 2:5, 8; 3:5). But Rom. 3:25 affirms, when we could never bring about our own acceptance by works, or what we could give (1 Pet. 1:18 is clear – we are not ransomed "with perishable things such as silver or gold."), God in love took the initiative and his son was "put forward as a propitiation by his blood." The concept of propitiation is about the removal of wrath. Christ paid the price for us on the cross and we can be delivered from the wrath of God. Instead of wrath we can be "justified by faith" and have "peace with God through our Lord Jesus Christ," (Rom. 5:1). This peace in not a changing emotion – one day here and the next day gone – it is about being brought into a new relationship of peace with God, which does not change. But there is more for that precious blood is:

BLOOD THAT CLEANSES

This is the wonderful promise of 1 John 1:7. John in his first epistle has to emphasize the reality of sin, for there were those who claimed they had "no sin" and had "not sinned," (1 John 1:8, 10). The situation was that certain people associated with the church had left it, ("they went out from us," 2v19). The reason was the influence of Gnosticism which was just beginning to become more developed. The Gnostics claimed that matter is evil and spirit is good. The body is matter, therefore the body is evil. But there is a divine spark imprisoned in man. Through secret knowledge only for the initiated, one can escape the body and have communion with God. The heresy produced different effects in the Christian community in 1 John. One was an ethical effect, with the teaching that the body does not matter at all. You can let your desires be indulged to the full. Purity and morality are unimportant and do not affect your spirit. John's answer was to emphasise that God is absolutely holy, "God is light and in him is no darkness at all," (1:5). To claim to "have fellowship with him" and still "walk in darkness" is to lie. John makes things clear again in 2:3, "And by this we know that we have come to know him, if we keep his commandments," and in 3:9, "No-one born of God makes a practice of sinning, for God's seed abides in him, and he cannot keep on sinning because he has been born of God." Those who left the church and had adopted this "freedom" of lifestyle were deceived. God was intrinsically holy and their actions were sinful – in fact as he states in 3:8, "Whoever makes a practice of sinning is of the devil." Again, "whoever does not practice righteousness is not of God," (3:10).

So sin is real and deadly. This was why the Son of God came. God sent him to be "the propitiation for our sins," (4:10) – to take our place, to bear the wrath for us; and to be "the Savior of the world," (4:14). So in 1:7 John announces what Christ can do for us through his sacrifice. "The blood of Jesus his Son cleanses us from all sin." The true apostolic faith, from which some have sadly departed while it emphasises the reality and seriousness of sin, also proclaims the all-sufficient answer in the death of Jesus, the cleansing from "all sin" that comes through his precious blood. But that blood has accomplished more. It is:

BLOOD THAT BRINGS US TO HEAVEN

In Rev. 5:9-10 John was caught up in the Spirit into heaven. The Lamb is enthroned there and takes the scroll from the hand of God. The seven churches of chapter 2 and 3, facing increasing persecution, were reminded that the future of the world which is revealed in the scroll is in his hands. Praise the Lord! The twenty-four elders fall down before him and there sounds out "the new song," to the Lamb. "Worthy are you...for you were slain, and by your blood you ransomed people for God from every tribe and language and people and nation," (5:9-10). So it is the blood which brings the ransomed to heaven.

On one occasion Oswald J. Smith was called to the bedside of a lady in the last stages of consumption. As he conversed with her she told him that she and her husband owned a shop for many years. They had never done anything wrong throughout all of their business dealings, always treating people fairly and honestly; no-one could say anything different about them. It was clear to him that all that she was relying on were their good deeds. He asked her what she knew about heaven and learned that she did not know a great deal about it, except that there would be singing. He turned to this passage in Rev. 5 and explained that those who were singing do NOT boast of anything they had done which brought them there. It was of the Lamb they sang, "You are worthy!" and THE PRECIOUS BLOOD was the means of their acceptance in heaven itself. They were NOT worthy to be there but it was his death for them which opened the way for them. They could testify, as John could testify, "Jesus Christ...has freed us from our sins by his blood," (1:5). The blood and only the blood brings us to heaven. All that need to be done for guilty sinners, he has done. If we repent of our way of sin and independence, put our trust in him, we can be set free from the condemnation of our sins and accepted.

Finally, it is:

BLOOD THAT SEALS OUR DESTINY

In Heb.10:29 the author writes of the contrast between the one who "has set aside the law of Moses," (10:28) and was judged severely for it, with the one who "has spurned the Son of God, and has profaned the blood of the covenant," who would face an even greater judgment. The problem was that certain individuals having been challenged by the Christian gospel had attached themselves to the church. But they were suffering; they had "endured a hard struggle with sufferings, sometimes being publically exposed to reproach and affliction" and the author reveals the cost of identifying with Christ, "you joyfully accepted the plundering of your property," (10:32-34). They were being tempted to just go back to the temple, the sacrifices still being offered there and to the old priesthood. They needed to realize what this would mean. The epistle has been emphasizing that the old perpetual sacrifices had been replaced by the sacrifice "for all time" (10:12) offered by Christ on the cross and the Christian's High Priest was now seated in heaven - not in Jerusalem or in the temple. Rather than retrace their steps to the temple, they now had access "into the holiest" and to a risen and exalted Jesus who would "sympathize" and give them "grace to help" in every trial and would be there "able to help those who were being tempted," (Heb. 2:17-18; 4:14-16; 10:19-25).

What would it mean for someone to turn back to the Judaism of old? In effect they would be saying that Jesus was only an imposter, not the true messiah and his blood was not the blood of the new covenant but only common blood! They would have "profaned the blood of the covenant," (10:29) and would be open to "a fearful expectation of judgment," (10:27). But the writer was certain of one thing and could affirm, "Though we speak in this way, yet in your case, beloved, we feel sure of better things – things that belong to salvation," (6:9). Those truly saved would not turn back but would endure.

In conclusion we also must see ourselves in the light of this situation. We may sit in various churches, even read religious books and commentaries, but to turn away from Christ and his precious blood is to turn away from "the blood of the covenant," and only in the covenant can one find new birth, with the law written upon our hearts, and forgiveness, when God "will remember their sins and their lawless deeds no more," (10:16-17). The precious blood is blood that seals our destiny for it reminds us of a sacrifice which was once for all time. When we repent or turn from our sin, put all our trust in Christ and in his precious blood, it is blood "that speaks a better word" than the blood of Abel. Here is certain hope.

CHAPTER FOURTEEN

Hope to Start Again

Ruth 1:1-22

I HAVE YET to meet someone who has gone through all of life without having regrets. For many "if only" has become a way of life. In Gethsemane, when Jesus found his disciples sleeping, he could warn them, "Watch and pray that you may not enter into temptation. The spirit indeed is willing, but the flesh is weak," (Matt. 26:41). We have not always "watched" for there are times when the flesh has claimed the victory. Paul could also say in Rom. 7:19 "For I do not do the good I want, but the evil I do not want is what I keep on doing."

There have been times when even great saints have fallen. Abraham in Gen. 16:1-6 with Hagar as he tried to help God with the almighty's promise of descendants; Moses in striking the rock (Num. 20:11); David with Bathsheba (2 Sam. 11:2-5) and Peter in denying Christ in the High Priest's palace (John 18:15-27). Times when we would have wished we had the opportunity to live the day over again. Alas, we cannot. Yet we know that God is the God of the second chance. There is hope and we can start again! We can see this in the case of Naomi. The title of the message I preached a few times, based on Ruth 1, was "Coming Home at Harvest-Time." Naomi could admit in 1:21 "I went away full and the Lord has brought me back empty". It may be that once you walked with God, knew his blessing and power, but you drifted away in heart, missed the way, took a wrong step and lost out with God. The message of this chapter is that you can have a new beginning; you can start again. As Naomi you can come home at harvest-time.

The book of Ruth is a link between the time of the Judges and the Kings. Compare Judges 21:25 which closes with the reference that there was "no king in Israel" and Ruth 4:22 where "David" is now mentioned. There was a very sad state of things in the time of the Judges, with the lives of people neither governed nor guided by the word of God. "Everyone did what was right in his own eyes," (Jud. 21:25). How are our lives being governed? Are you also doing just what we want to do, regardless of what we read in God's word or hear from the pulpit - what is right in our own eyes? Let us trace the movements of Naomi.

GOING OUT TO MOAB

How did Naomi end up leaving Bethlehem to go "to sojourn in the country of Moab"? Well we also note that 1:1 says "a man of Bethlehem in Judah went," but in 1:21 when Naomi relates her bitter experience and all that happened she confesses "I went away." She had been the big influence in the decision as Elimelech, her husband, with her sons, Mahlon and Chilion all went with her from Bethlehem.

Why did the family go to Moab? In 1:1 we learn that "In the days when the judges ruled there was a famine in the land." The nature of the country, with the rugged hills and hot climate without much rainfall and perennial streams made it particularly susceptible to drought. It was dependant on the periodic rains and if these were withheld there was no river as in Egypt to take their place. But it was clearly a wrong step for them as a family. What does 1:6 say brought her back? It was food. "Then she arose with her daughters-in-law to return from the country of Moab, for she had heard in the fields of Moab that the LORD had visited his people and given them food." But that was what took her out! What did this move to Moab involve for Naomi? For her there was:

DEPARTURE

In the past it was clear that a famine was a call to repent. We think of the promise of 2 Chron. 7:14, "If my people who are called by my name humble themselves, and pray and seek my face and turn from their wicked ways, then I will hear from heaven and will forgive their sin and heal their land." In spite of the awful spiritual state of Judah in the time of the judges there appears to have been no repentance or crying to God. This seems to be the case also here with Naomi and the whole family. There was no repentance in her heart, no seeking of God, no closeness and no prayer to God for this great move from Bethlehem.

DISTRUST
God sometimes tested the faith of his people in famine. But with Naomi, she, rather than trusting God, extracted herself and her whole family from the circumstances. Soon things went wrong in this move to Moab.

DISTRESS
In 1:3 we learn that her husband Elimelech "died, and she was left…" When you are out of his will, out of the path God has for you, things can go wrong. We accept that sometimes when bereavement comes it may not be because of sin; but in this case, the whole way the story is narrated, plus the confession Naomi makes on her return (see below) would clearly imply that the things that happened were evidence of judgment.

DISOBEDIENCE
The name Elimelech has the meaning "God is my king." Did this reflect where things had been in the past with this family and God? No more! Her two sons entered into marriages which would be clearly outside the will of God. The names of the young men were Mahlon "sick" and Chilion "pining" which in this situation is surely meant to reflect spiritually the state of their hearts. Their wives are named as Orpah and Ruth. Marriage outside the faith of Israel will imply that pagan influences would become dominant in their homes. This is

reflected in the words of Naomi later about Orpah, as her daughter-in-law drew back from going with her when she was about to return to the land of Israel. She said to Ruth, "See, your sister-in-law has gone back to her people and to her gods…" (1:15). It seems clear that the relationships these young men entered into were meant to reflect that they were in opposition to the will of God.

DISASTER

In vv. 4-5 we learn that when they had lived there approximately ten years both her sons died! Naomi had experienced nothing but trouble and loss when she initiated this move to Moab. The story is surely giving evidence of the fact that she was away from God and in rebellion as far as his will was concerned. When Naomi is on her way back from Moab she acknowledges that in the deciding to leave Bethlehem and all that had ensued, "the hand of the LORD has gone out against me," (1:13). Also when she has returned to Bethlehem she confesses that God has dealt with her severely. "I went away full, and the LORD has brought me back empty. Why call me Naomi, when the LORD has testified against me and the Almighty has brought calamity upon me?" (1:21).

The things which are recorded here in Ruth has the same message for us as other narratives in the OT. "Now the things happened to them as an example, but they were written down for our instruction, on whom the end of the ages has come," (1 Cor. 10:11). Can you identify with any of this? Praise God it is not the end, as the whole story reflects. God in his kindness and mercy can allow us to pick up the broken pieces of our lives. We can start again for he is the God of the second chance. He can bring us out of the dark shadows.

We should remember that many of the things that happened to Elimelech and his family happened to the people of Israel when they disobeyed God after entering the promised land: crop failure and barrenness (Deut. 28:18); drought (Deut. 28: 23-24) and removal from the land (Deut. 28:36). Also note that after the exile when the remnant had returned, the Lord still chastened his people for their neglect of the spiritual e.g., Haggai 1:6 "You have sown much, and harvested little. You eat, but you never have enough; you drink, but you never have your fill. You clothe yourselves, but no one is warm. And he who earns wages does so to put them into a bag with holes." Again God challenges his people in Mal. 3:11 that if they turn to him with all their hearts, he would "rebuke the devourer" for them so that the fruits of the soil and the vine in the field would yield a harvest. So here Naomi and her household experience difficult times which reflect how far they were from God at this time. But as with them, so with us, all such experiences are meant to cause us to reflect upon our disobedience and turn again to him. As Heb. 12:5-13 teaches, when we are disciplined, God's intention is not that we should regard it lightly or faint under it (v.5), but seek to learn from it and why God has sent it i.e., to profit or be "trained" from it (v.11).

Now as far as Naomi is concerned, as we will see, in the midst of these distressing circumstances and punishments, God cares for her and displays grace to both her and also Ruth. Later in the book Naomi sees how God has not cast her aside because of all that had happened in the past. In 2:17-23 she discovers how God has worked to bring Ruth to glean in the very field of Boaz "a close relative of ours, one of our redeemers" and gives thanks to the Lord "whose kindness has not forsaken the living and the dead!" (2:20). What a great God we have, a God of compassion, mercy and love. If you can see something of your own situation in the experiences of Naomi, again the message is clear, there is hope to start again.

RETURNING BACK TO JUDAH

Naomi learns in 1:6-7 that "the LORD had visited his people and given them food." If "the LORD" as the text says was the one who gave his people food, he must also have been the one who sent the famine. Now reflecting upon her tragic circumstances and her bitter experiences we are told that "she arose with her daughters-in-law to return from the country of Moab." She is going home again to the place she should never have left. If we have also strayed in some way from God, the time comes in life when we will have to retrace our steps. Remember that in an earlier chapter we referred to Abram who forsook the land of Canaan in a similar situation of famine. In Gen. 12:10 "Abram went down to Egypt to sojourn there, for the famine was severe in the land." A wrong move for the one who in faith had only recently come to Canaan from Haran. We noted that the day came when he had to retrace his steps. In 13:1-4 Abram "went up from Egypt" and journeyed to Bethel. This was the place where he had formally pitched his tent and had made an altar at the first. We are told "there Abram called upon the name of the Lord."

Therefore we learn that when one faces failure, it is possible to start again. But we must also acknowledge that when we are out of God's way and will, things can happen and there can often be consequences which we will have to live with. For example it was apparently during Abram's time in Egypt that Sarai acquired her "Egyptian" servant Hagar, who later became the mother of Ishmael (16:1, 15). Also when David was challenged by Nathan the prophet about his adultery with Bathsheba and confessed his sin, while the Lord forgave him, he was warned by Nathan of the lasting consequences, "Now therefore the sword shall never depart from your house, because you have despised me, and have taken the wife of Uriah the Hittite to be your wife," (2 Sam. 12:10). So when we stray, God can graciously forgive us and restore; but sometimes there are consequences from our sin – here David's family was greatly affected e.g., 2 Sam. 13:1-33, the killing of David's son Amnon by Absalom for the violation of Tamar his sister. Yet, thank God we can start again.

In this account of Naomi, Orpah and Ruth again we see the negative influence of a believer out of touch with God. The two girls had accompanied her on her homeward journey (the oriental parting never took place within the home. When a guest was leaving they were always accompanied some way along the road). But it seems that they were intent on going with her into Judah. It is clear that Naomi was not yet restored in her own soul. She was no help to them. She tells them to go back to their own people and gods! "But Naomi said to her two daughters-in-law in 1:8-9, 'Go, return each of you to her mother's house...The Lord grant that you may find rest, each of you in the house of her husband!'" She knew all that was implied here, as later we noted in v.15, she refers to Orpha who went back "to her people and to her gods." When away from God there was no real spirituality of mind, no vision, no recognition that these girls needed to come to know the LORD the God of Israel "under whose wings" (2:12) they could take refuge. So there was no concern for their spiritual welfare. Was having a husband and a home was all that mattered! What about the future families of these girls from such a union in Moab? Naomi's attitude or her concerns are reflected again so often today. In our modern families, are we really concerned for the things that matter above all? There are times when parents are more passionate about the education of their children and their success in this world than they are for their souls! Where are we spiritually? Orpah went back to her people, but Ruth clung to Naomi. With her there was evidence of faith. "Do not urge me to leave you or return from following you. For where you go I will go, and where you lodge I will lodge. Your people shall be my people, and your God my God. Where you die I will die, and there will I be buried. May the LORD do so to me and more also if anything but death parts me from you," (1:16-17). It must have been a real challenge to Naomi when she saw the perseverance of Ruth.

COMING HOME TO BETHLEHEM

In 1:19-22 Naomi admits her sinful failure. She acknowledges that she and her family took a wrong step, as we noted. "Do not call me Naomi (pleasant); call me Mara (bitter), for the Almighty has dealt very bitterly with me," (1:20). She has been brought back "empty". She admits her awful mistake, her rebellion, disobedience. There is real regret! It is clear that she also humbles herself.

Sometimes we take a wrong step, make a wrong decision. We have not sought the Lord about the path we have taken. Have you gone wrong, disobeyed and shut out God and his will? The story before us reassures us that we can humbly come home to God and confess our sin.

God is a gracious God. When we are prepared to sincerely acknowledge that we have gone wrong then God can act. He did for Naomi – and in fact Ruth. God is a merciful God and he still cared about Naomi and had a glorious purpose for her in his grace. We first need to note how in 2:1-2 Ruth will not just sit without helping her mother-in-law. She requests that she might go to glean for some ears of grain after the reapers of the harvest. So we are told "she happened to come to the part of the field belonging to Boaz," (2:3). But the question is what the author of the book meant by "happened to come"? It is clear that God was sovereignly at work in the whole situation in his glorious grace! Boaz was "of the clan of Elimelech." Here was a kinsman who would be their redeemer! We listen to Naomi in 2:19-20 as she confesses that the Lord has not forsaken his kindness to the living and the dead – to her and her daughter-in-law. The kinsman redeemer was willing and able to redeem! We note how the goodness of God continues in 4:9-10, "Then Boaz said to the elders and all the people, 'You are witnesses this day that I have bought from the hand of Naomi all that belonged to Elimelech and all that belonged to Chilion and to Mahlon. Also Ruth the Moabite, the widow of Mahon, I have bought to be my wife, to perpetuate the name of the dead in his inheritance, that the name of the dead may not be cut off from among his brothers and from the gate of his native place. You are witnesses this day.'" What a redemption for Naomi and Ruth!

So God in his mercy and grace sovereignly works out his redemptive plan. Soon a son is born to Boaz and Ruth. Their son is not merely an heir of Naomi. The son, Obed, becomes the father of Jesse, who is the father of David (4:17). Thus Obed begins the Davidic line, which will eventually bring David to the throne. But there is more; David's greater Son, Jesus Christ (Matt. 1:5-6), would become the redeemer of all God's people. The women of Bethlehem said to Naomi, "Blessed be the LORD, who has not left you this day without a redeemer, and may his name be renowned in Israel! He shall be to you a restorer of life and a nourisher of your old age, for your daughter-in-law who loves you, who is more to you that seven sons, has given birth to him," 4:14-15.

What mercy, what grace God showed to Naomi. Her sorrow and pain was turned to joy. The dark shadows of the past are behind her. She was given a whole new life, a new start. God can do this. There is hope to start again. He can remove the deep shadows of sin and sorrow that can envelop our lives – if we turn again to him in confession, acknowledging our failure and disobedience, if we retrace our steps. There is hope to start again.

CHAPTER FIFTEEN

Hope in Christ's Coming

1 Thess. 1:10

PAUL WRITES TO the young church in Thessalonica on hearing the news Timothy has brought back to him from that city when the apostle had moved on in his missionary effort to Athens. The planting of the church in Thessalonica is set out in Acts 17:1-10. God had worked in a remarkable way as Paul on three Sabbath days in the synagogue "reasoned with them from the Scriptures," (v.2). Some of the Jews were persuaded, also "a great many of the devout Greeks and not a few of the leading women," (v.4). The Jews of Thessalonica were jealous of the success of the gospel and with the help of "some wicked men of the rabble, they formed a mob, set the city in an uproar," (v.5). They criticized the apostles to the city authorities – really in quite remarkable terms – "These men who have turned the world upside down have come here also," (v.6). The "brothers" in the newly formed church decided it was best to let the missionaries leave. So Paul, having gone on to Berea and Athens, now "when he could bear it no longer… sent Timothy…" (1 Thess. 3:1-2) and having learned how things were back in Thessalonica, writes this letter.

It is in 1 Thess. 1:9-10 that Paul sets out how God had worked among the people in Thessalonica. There was REAL CONVERSION "you turned to God from idols" LOVING DEDICATION "to serve the living and true God," and then DAILY EXPECTATION "to wait for his Son from heaven, whom he raised from the dead." The Greek word "wait" means to wait with patience, with confident expectation. This is the hope about which there is no uncertainty. He IS surely coming, actually, physically, bodily. Acts 1:11 affirmed, "This Jesus, who was taken up from you into heaven, will come in the same way as you saw him go into heaven."

In 2 Peter 3 the apostle reminds us that scoffers will come in the last days who will say, "Where is the promise of his coming? For ever since the fathers fell asleep, all things are continuing as they were from the beginning of creation," (3:3-4). Michael Green[24] has given us an excellent summary of Peter's response to this denial of Christ's coming upon which we now draw. He points out that Peter argues for the certainty of Christ's coming from history, the manner in which the Lord reckons time in Scripture and from the character of God. First, those who claim that all things have continued unchanged from the creation have forgotten the flood. "For they deliberately overlook this fact, that the heavens existed long ago, and the earth was formed out of water and through water by the word of God." Now Peter reminds us that God did intervene in judgment "the world that then existed was deluged with water and perished," (v. 5-6). In a moral world sin will not forever go unpunished. God will intervene again, not this time by water but "by the same word, the heavens and earth that now exist are stored up for fire, being kept until the day of judgment and the destruction of the ungodly," (v.7).

Secondly, the Lord does not reckon time as we do. He alludes to Psa. 90:4,[25] "But do not overlook this one fact, beloved, that with the Lord one day is as a thousand years, and a thousand years as one day," (v.8). And finally, we need to remember the longsuffering nature of the character of God. "The Lord is not slow to fulfil his promise as some count slowness, but is patient toward you, not wishing that any should perish, but that all should reach repentance," (v.9). Therefore, the only reason why Christ has not come and tarried at the throne, is just his

---

[24] M. Green, *2 Peter and Jude*, (Leicester: Inter-Varsity Press, 2003), 140-152.

[25] Psa. 90:4 "For a thousand years in your sight are but as when it is past, or as a watch in the night."

longsuffering. But Peter affirms that in spite of the scoffers, "The day of the Lord will come like a thief…" (v.10), and we must be ready.

Therefore in the light of Christ's coming, it is important to consider what Paul has to say here about that coming. How does Paul encourage and challenge the young church in Thessalonica? They "wait" for God's son from heaven; but what are they waiting for? We are waiting for some wonderful blessings. Some of them are highlighted here in this epistle and elsewhere in the NT Scriptures.

WAITING FOR THE GLORIFICATION 1:10

The son, who "was raised" and who is coming again, is the one who "delivers us from the wrath to come," (v.10). Rather than "wrath" or damnation, we experience glorification! As sinners by nature and by practice we were hell-deserving. We have already noted Isa. 53:6 which makes this clear. "All we like sheep have gone astray," because of our fallenness we wandered away from God and his will and way. "we have turned – every one – to his own way." We put self on the throne of our lives and dethroned God. We were rebels. We truly deserve judgment! As Paul said in Eph. 2:12, we had "no hope" and were "without God in the world." Isa. 53:6 also reveals, how for helpless sinners God himself in love acted for us, "the LORD has laid upon him the iniquity of us all." Jesus, the Servant of the Lord became accountable! By his death on the cross, all who "believe" (Isa. 53:1) can by God's grace be accepted, forgiven and as Paul writes here can all be delivered from the wrath to come – glorification, rather than damnation. Praise the Lord! But we can wait for more than this. Paul writes of:

WAITING FOR THE JUBILATION 2:19-20

In 2:17-18 Paul reminds them that he and his companions were "torn away" from them. But it was "in person, not in heart." He so wanted to get back to see them again but "Satan hindered us," we are unsure how. He writes of how much they meant to him, then focuses upon the return of the Lord. "For what is our hope or joy or crown of boasting before our Lord Jesus at his coming? Is it not you? For you are our glory and joy." Paul was saying first of all that the presence of his converts in heaven was giving evidence of their real election by God as 1:4 had affirmed. They had persevered. But did it also provide assurance concerning the reality of their teachers - Paul and his companions as well? In addition, the converts from Thessalonica would bring Paul a "crown" and the "joy" that his service had not been in vain.

The question is will we also have anything in our lives to warrant a reward and will we be able to rejoice? I recall a challenging solo from the past which impacted my early life. "How many are the lost that I have lifted? How many of the chained I've helped to free?" Thinking again of 2 Peter 3, one should note vv.11-12. "Since all these things are thus to be dissolved, what sort of people ought you to be in lives of holiness and godliness, waiting for and hastening the coming of the day of God..." It seems clear that the phrase in v. 12 is not about "hastening unto" as it is also translated, but rather "hastening" the coming itself! But how can one hasten the second coming of Christ? Is this time not fixed in the plan and purpose of God? No doubt this is so. The challenge here is about so dedicating our lives to God, so allowing him to take us and use us that God's actual purpose is hastened and fulfilled. The challenge is to let God have his way as we put ourselves more and more in his hands that he may hasten the gathering in of his redeemed people! If we commit ourselves to the work of the kingdom, then we as well as Paul will know something of this jubilation about which he writes.

WAITING FOR THE CONFIRMATION 3:12-13
Paul reminds the believers at Thessalonica of the importance of love for one another. Was there some evidence reaching him through Timothy of behaviour to the contrary? He urges "may the Lord make you increase and abound in love for one another and for all..." (v.12).

Later in 5:12-15 there are a number of statements which reflect again Paul's concern for unity among them and that they show evidence of real love one for the other. He calls upon the believers to "respect those who labor among you and are over you in the Lord…esteem them very highly in love because of their work." He exhorts them to "Be at peace among yourselves…See that no one repays anyone evil for evil, but always seek to do good to one another and to everyone." Making sure that one develops such love and this response to each other, as Paul urges here, is vital for the advancement of the work but also to be pleasing to the Lord.

Sadly, we live in an age when believers can demonstrate malice, hostility, and bitterness towards one another yet at the same time profess to be holy and blameless before God. It needs to be stressed today that to manifest such evil attitudes as we have just mentioned, while claiming to have a relationship with God, is to be self-deceived. It is here in 1 Thess. 3 that Paul can state to "abound in love for one another" provides the evidence of any claim to be "blameless in holiness before our God and Father at the coming of our Lord Jesus…" (3:12-13). The question is, will Christ's coming confirm that we are blameless in holiness? There may be different things in our lives which could confirm this at that moment. But one thing must not be lacking. The important point Paul is making is that anything other than the fact we are demonstrating the respect, esteem, patience, non-retaliation, acceptance and love that he calls for among believers in chapter five, will leave us without this confirmation. The basic question remains, is our behaviour hypocritical or holy? How real is our profession to belong to the God who is himself "love"? 1 John 4:8 affirms, "Anyone who does not love does not know God, because God is love."

WAITING FOR THE REUNION 4:13-14

It is clear that in the short time frame since Paul and the other missionaries had moved on, some of the believers had died. Timothy, who had come from Thessalonica as 3:2 reveals, will have reported this to Paul and the questions which had been raised because of it by those who have suffered loss of their loved ones and friends. This is why Paul writes "we do not want you to be uninformed brothers..." (v.13). Paul takes time to write to them of what had been revealed to him "by a word from the Lord," (v.15).

First he writes of THE SLEEP. "those who are asleep." When a believer dies the body sleeps, but not the soul. We know this to be true from other Scriptures like Ecclesiastes 12:7, which refers to the fact that at death "the spirit returns to God who gave it" and 2 Cor. 5:8, highlighted in an earlier chapter, when Paul assures us that we would be "away from the body and at home with the Lord." Again, we noted earlier that Rev. 6:9-10 refers to the souls under the altar who "cried out with a loud voice..." So at death it is only the body which sleeps and of course, when we sleep we wake again – as Paul reveals about "the dead in Christ" at the second coming.

Paul is also aware of THE SORROW. He knows that they "grieve" (v.13) for their loved ones. Even Jesus wept at the grave of Lazarus in John 11:35, because of his love for him and in the face of the reality of what sin and the fall have brought. So it is not sinful to grieve. Paul acknowledges that we grieve, but not "as others who have no hope." Note in passing that death settles our destiny! It is so important to be ready when this moment comes. It is possible to be in a state where we are facing death and have "no hope" and are "without God in the world," Eph. 2:12. We must seriously consider where we are going in eternity. To be ready for his coming we need to be as Paul says "in Christ" (4:16) the one who died for sinners and rose again. It is in him, not in ourselves, as we noted earlier, that we must trust. It is "through Jesus" (4:14) that God will bring them again with him. There is a well-known story of the old Scottish shepherd who was visited by the local minister as he lay seriously ill and not likely to recover. When asked about his spiritual condition and his relationship with God he assured his pastor, "I thatched my house before the storm came."[26]   How vital it is to be ready, first for the moment of death, but also for the moment of his coming again!

For one day there will be the SHOUT. "For the Lord himself" – this is not some kind of "spiritual" coming, for he is coming himself. We are told that he "will descend from heaven with a cry of command, with the voice of an archangel, and with the sound of the trumpet of God. And the dead in Christ will rise first," (4:16).

Then the SHARING. "Then we who are alive, who are left, will be caught up together with them in the clouds to meet the Lord in the air." We meet each other – we are "caught up together with them" - and then we meet the Lord. Note this clearly. First the dead in Christ are raised. Paul makes the point that the resurrection of Christ was also the assurance that God would raise his people. "For since we believe that Jesus died and rose again, even so, through Jesus, God will bring with him those who have fallen asleep," (4:14). Then the bodies of those living will be transformed to be caught up with them.

Then there is SOLACE. "so we will always be with the Lord. Therefore encourage one another with these words," (4:17-18). What a future at the second coming of the Lord. What comfort in the sorrow of bereavement. But note that we have to be with the Lord here first, in a personal saving relationship, if we are going to be "with the Lord" then. Turning from the Thessalonian letter to the Johannine epistle we learn that we are also:

WAITING FOR THE TRANSFORMATION 1 John 3:2-10
John in his epistle writes of the unfathomable love of God in making us his children. He then emphasises the fact, "Beloved, we are God's children now, and what we will be has not yet appeared; but we know that when he appears we shall be like him, because we shall see him as

---

[26]   I saw the quote recently again in Cecil A. Newell *Pilgrims on a Journey in Company*, Part 3, (Belfast, 2014), 253.

he is," (3:2). What a glorious prospect to be like him when he comes! But what John wishes to emphasise is that this transformation starts here, now in the present. Every man who has this expectation "purifies himself" already "as he is pure," (v.3).

We have already noted the influence of Gnosticism which was just beginning to develop and had caused some to withdraw from the apostolic community, (2:19). The Gnostics believed that matter was evil, including the body - although there was a divine spark imprisoned in man. Through secret knowledge only for the initiated, it would become possible to "escape" the body and have communion with God. We noted earlier that in 1 John the Gnostics were therefore teaching that in fact the body does not matter at all nor affect the spirit and therefore a person's desires could be indulged to the full. John has in mind the heresy here when he stresses that if we will be totally transformed and made holy like him at the coming of the Lord, the child of God now already should be seeking to purify himself, (3:3). He proceeds to set out further arguments for holiness of life. In v. 4 he emphasises that practising sin is practising lawlessness. It transgresses God's law. Again, this is the reason why Christ came in the first place, "You know that he appeared to take away sins" and he also himself is holy, "in him there is no sin", (3:5) – how then can we practice it? John emphasises that abiding in him will deliver from it and in fact righteousness is a sign that we truly belong to God. As we noted earlier in a previous chapter, "No-one born of God makes a practice of sinning, for God's seed abides in him, and he cannot keep on sinning because he has been born of God," (3:9). Let the transformation begin!

WAITING FOR THE COMMENDATION Matt. 25:14-21

In the parable of the talents Jesus tells of the one servant who had zealously used the five talents he was given. A "talent" was estimated to be a financial sum in value equal to twenty years wages for a labouring man. The time came for the reckoning, when the Master came and "settled accounts with them," (25:19). The question first is, are we servants? Do we obey our Master? Do we submit to his word? In 1 Thess. 2:13 Paul can write of his converts in Thessalonica, "we also thank God constantly for this, that when you received the word of God, which you heard from us, you accepted it not as the word of men but as what it really is, the word of God, which is at work in you believers."

Again, have we any work for him? In Rev. 22:12 Jesus reminds us, "Behold, I am coming soon, bringing my recompense with me, to repay everyone for what he has done." In 1 Cor. 1:7 Paul can acknowledge of the Corinthians "you are not lacking in any spiritual gift, as you wait for the revealing of our Lord Jesus Christ." But are we using those gifts or are we burying them in the sand? We must not forget 2 Cor. 5:10 that the day to "settle accounts" will come, "For we must all appear" – none are excluded – "before the judgment seat of Christ, so that each one may receive what is due for what he has done in the body, whether good or evil." Will there be commendation or will we experience something of what John writes in 1 John 2:28? "And now, little children, abide in him, so that when he appears we may have confidence and not shrink away from him in shame at his coming." So will it be commendation or shame? But there is more for we are:

WAITING FOR THE REVELATION John 13:7
One recalls the gathering in the Upper Room with "his own" before he went out to Gethsemane and to Calvary in John 13:1-31. As an example for them of service and humility he performs the menial task of the servant washing the disciples' feet, dusty from the journey. Peter of course protests, "Lord, do you wash my feet?" Jesus replies, "What I am doing you do not understand now, but afterward you will understand," (v.7). This text has often brought comfort and hope to those who are in an unexpected trial. Things can happen suddenly and without warning, causing us to experience a difficult time of testing of

our faith. The dark shadows of life can close in around us with a devastating effect. Here at this time Jesus speaks of "What I am doing." Jesus is doing something in our lives every day; he is working out his purpose. We may not see what he is doing at the moment and we may never see it in this life. Here he says, "afterward you will understand." We noted earlier the words of Job in Job 23:10, "But he knows the way that I take; when he has tried me I shall come out as gold." The fires of the crucible purifies the gold. Again, the tapestry will display a pattern of perfection and beauty; yet the other side will be a mass of tangled threads. We only see the twisted, untidy threads and we have to trust him in the darkness of our situation and confusion. But afterward we will understand, when he comes and we are with him, then he will make it all clear. God does not cause his child a needless tear. Paul reminds us in 1 Cor. 13:12, "For now we see in a mirror dimly, but then face to face. Now I know in part; then shall I know fully, even as I have been fully known." The full revelation is yet to come. We trust when we do not see or understand why. We turn our faces toward the 'son' and the shadows are behind us.

In the new heaven and the new earth as it was revealed to John we are assured, "Behold, the dwelling place of God is with man. He will dwell with them, and they will be his people, and God himself will be with them as their God. He will wipe away every tear from their eyes, and death shall be no more, neither shall there be mourning, nor crying, nor pain anymore, for the former things have passed away," Rev. 21:3-4. Trust him in the darkness, when you do not understand why. Finally, we are:

WAITING FOR THE REDEMPTION. Rom. 8:18-25

In Rom. 8:18 Paul assures the believers that, "For I consider that the sufferings of this present time are not worth comparing with the glory that is to be revealed to us." The passage that follows is really an expansion of the glory that is before at the second coming of our Lord

Jesus Christ. We find a broadening out of God's purposes beyond Israel and the Gentile believers to the whole of creation. Romans 8 is about life in the indwelling Spirit and here there is the theme of hope. As we noted at the beginning, secular hope has the element of risk; biblical hope is marked by security and certainty. The reason why this hope is reliable is that it is founded upon God and his promises.

Paul continues by referring to "creation"; by this he means the whole of the created world. This creation is waiting "with eager longing" for "the revealing of the sons of God." This revealing is explained shortly. But now in v.20 he states, "For the creation was subjected to futility, not willingly, but because of him who subjected it, in hope." The meaning is that God subjected all things to Adam, including his creation; God then subjected the creation to fallen Adam, to share in his fallenness. This is how we understand the statement "not willingly." It was subjected not by its own choice, because Adam was to blame and the judgment was from God. It was subjected to "futility," which means that it does not fulfil what it was designed to do. It was subjected "in hope," affirming that the future involves the reversal of the curse and creation restored to fulfil its true purpose. And what a future is here in v.21! "the creation itself will be set free from its bondage to corruption and obtain the freedom of the glory of the children of God."

Through the teaching of the apostles the believers knew that creation "has been groaning together in the pains of childbirth," v.22. We should note that Paul writes not about creation suffering death pangs but birth-pangs! The world has a great future and so have God's children! Is there any guarantee that we should hope for such a glorious future? Yes, since "we have the firstfruits of the Spirit," or the firstfruits, "which is the Spirit," i.e., the indwelling Holy Spirit, (v.23). In the OT the term "firstfruits" referred to what the farmer gave to God ahead of the harvest; in this passage it is about what God gives to us ahead of the full blessing to be ours in the future. As Paul puts it here, we "groan inwardly as we wait eagerly for adoption as sons, the redemption of our bodies," (v. 23).

So we have been caught up in the groaning that characterizes all of creation. We live in a broken world since the fall, with all of its earthquakes and tsunamis. Our bodies also become weak, subject to sickness and disease. But one day Christ will come and we will be liberated (as creation in the future will also be). We are already adopted, as v.15 states, "For you did not receive the spirit of slavery to fall back into fear, but you have received the Spirit of adoption as sons, by whom we cry 'Abba! Father!'" But at the moment of his coming we will enter into the full experience of our sonship with God.

In v24-25 we learn that the Christian life is already characterised by that steadfast hope or certainty of that glory which has not yet been fully revealed. "Now hope that is seen is not hope. For who hopes for what he sees? But if we hope for what we do not see, we wait for it with patience." It is true that you cannot hope for or anticipate something you already see. But we can look forward to something that is certain – which is what true Biblical hope really is - and let it influence our lives today. So the Lord's return is certain. Paul is saying that we can endure what life throws at us, the dark clouds of sadness, the shadows which may envelop us, as we wait for our full redemption.

Until then we obey the saviour's exhortation, "Stay dressed for action and keep your lamps burning, and be like men who are waiting for their master to come home..." Luke 12:35-36. Are we expecting him? Are we sons of God now already? Will our bodies be redeemed? Are we yet among those who have been delivered from the wrath to come? As Isa. 55:6-7 exhorts us, "Seek the Lord while he may be found; call upon him while he is near." There will come a time when he will no longer be found or when he will no longer be near. Therefore, without delay, "let the wicked forsake his way, and the unrighteous man his thoughts; let him return to the Lord, that he may have compassion upon him, and to our God, for he will abundantly pardon." He is coming suddenly (1 Cor. 15:52) - in the twinkling of an eye!

Conclusion

JAMES WRITES OF the fact that believers will throughout life meet "trials of various kinds," (Jam. 1:2). Dark shadows will fall across our path. In facing such trials we will need an anchor; a rock upon which we can stand, or a light which will dispel the darkness. We need hope, but not an uncertain hope. There is only one place that we can find this certainty to enable us not to sink or go under emotionally and spiritually, as Peter was about physically to do as he walked upon the water to go to Jesus (Matt. 14:30). We can find this hope in the promises of God, in the Scriptures. We began this book by quoting from Paul in Rom. 15:4 "For whatever was written in former days was written for our instruction, that through endurance and through the encouragement of the Scriptures we might have hope." It is from God's word that we will find first assurance of our salvation and then the "comfort" or "encouragement" to endure in difficult days. Psa. 119:114 also states, "You are my hiding place and my shield; I hope in your word."

The purpose in writing this book is to assure you in the dark shadows of life when the threatening clouds surround you, your hope, your spirit can be renewed as you focus upon the word of God. The passages contained have been preached to different congregations throughout my ministry. I share my heart with you, praying the pages will be a torch of light in your darkness. May the Lord make these pages a blessing to you.

Charles Haddon Spurgeon[27] could write:

---

[27] Charles Haddon Spurgeon, *3 - Minute Devotions with Charles Spurgeon*, Uhrichsville, Ohio: Barbour Publishing Inc. 2015, 36. Used by permission.

We have many proverbs that remind us that men make light of one another's promises, and well they may; but we must never make light of the promises of God. "He spake, and it was done; he commanded, and it stood fast." So if there is a promise of God to help you in a time of trouble or to preserve you in the hour of temptation or to deliver you out of trial or to give you grace according to your day, that promise is as good as if it had been already performed, since God's Word shall certainly be followed by the fulfilment of it in due season.

John McArthur[28] when preaching on Psa. 42 told the story of a period in the eighties when his church was going through difficult times. The exhortations in this psalm, "Hope in God" (vv. 5, 11) meant so much to him and the whole congregation. They actually placed a "Hope in God" sign outside on the wall of the building and around the neighbourhood it became known as "The Hope Church." Is it possible that this description could also be used of you or your church? Have you grasped hold of the real hope that is ours in Jesus Christ?

The word of God will bring true hope to you, certainty, first for eternity and then in all the varied experiences of life. You have here promises to accept by faith that will enable you to experience God's salvation through his son and then to endure. In the dark shadows, read these promises, turn your eyes toward him and the shadows fall behind you.

---

[28] J. McArthur, "Spiritual Depression in the Psalms," June 1, 2008 in www.desiringgod.org accessed August 2017.